AS-Level

English

Language

The Revision Guide
Exam Board: AQA B

Rotherham College of Arts & Technology

R30582

Editors: Polly Cotterill, Rob MacDonald, Jennifer Underwood

Contributors: Najoud Ensaff, Tony Flanagan, Heather Haynes and Chris Reynolds

Proofreaders: Katherine Reed, Glenn Rogers and Elisabeth Sanderson

Published by Coordination Group Publications Ltd.

ISBN: 978 1 84762 143 6

Groovy website: www.cgpbooks.co.uk
Jolly bits of clipart from CorelDRAW®
Printed by Elanders Hindson Ltd, Newcastle upon Tyne.

Text, design, layout and original illustrations © Coordination Group Publications Ltd. 2008
All rights reserved.

Contents

THE LEARNING CENTRES
ACC No R30582
DATE 18/3/10
CLASS 420 COT

Language Frameworks

On the next two pages are the essential tools you need for describing and analysing spoken or written language.

You should aim to **Analyse** all **Texts** in a **Similar** way

If you have to analyse a piece of language or discourse, there are several things to think about:

1) **Genre** — **what kind** of language it is. Written discourses could be **instruction booklets** or **adverts**, and spoken discourses could be **formal speeches** to an audience or **casual conversations** between friends.

2) **Register** — a type of language that's appropriate for a particular audience or situation, e.g. the language of a political party or the language of the justice system. Register also includes the level of **formality** in a discourse.

3) **Audience** — the **listener** or **reader**. When you're analysing language, think about how the audience is **addressed**. It might be **formal** or **informal**, **direct** or **indirect**. For example, in advertising the audience is often directly addressed as *you*.

4) **Subject** — what the discourse is **about**. This will be reflected in the **lexical choices**, e.g. a discussion about healthy eating may contain words like *low-fat*, *diet*, and *nutrition*.

5) **Purpose** — what the speaker or writer is trying to **achieve** through language (e.g. to persuade, instruct, etc.).

6) **Mode** — whether the language is **written or spoken**. You can also get **mixed modes** — e.g. in text messages, where the language is written, but contains many of the informal features of spoken language.

There are **Seven Main Language Frameworks**

This table is an **overview** of what makes up each language framework (also called **linguistic frameworks**, or **toolkits**, and how they can be used. There are more detailed explanations of each one throughout the rest of the book.

Lexis	• **Lexis** means the **vocabulary** of a language — the total stock of words. • When you're analysing spoken and written language you'll notice words that share a **similar topic** or **focus**. For example, in an advert for mobile phones you'd find words such as *SMS*, *text-messaging*, and *battery life*. Words that are linked together in this way are known as a **lexical field**.
Semantics	• **Semantics** is the study of how **meaning** is created through words and phrases. Sometimes this meaning is **explicit**, but sometimes it's **implicit**. A word will have a **literal** meaning but it can also be **associated** with other meanings. • For example, the word *red* refers to a **colour**, but it can also be associated with **danger**.
Grammar	• **Grammar** is the system of **rules** that governs how phrases and sentences are **constructed**. There are two parts to this: 1) A system that **groups** words into classes according to their **function** (e.g. nouns or verbs). 2) A system of **rules** about how these types of words function in relation to each other (**syntax**).
Phonology	• **Phonology** is the study of **sounds** in English — how they're **produced** and how they're **combined** to make words. • This framework includes **Non-Verbal Aspects of Speech** (NVAS) or **prosody** — features of spoken language such as pace, stress, rhythm and intonation.
Pragmatics	• **Pragmatics** is sometimes called **language in use**. It's about how social conventions, context, personality and relationships influence the **choices** people make about their language. • For example, how you address other people shows **levels of formality** and **social conventions** — a student might address a teacher as *Miss Rogers* or *Lizzie* depending on what the college or school expects, and what the teacher finds acceptable.
Graphology	• **Graphology** is the study of the **appearance** of the writing and the effect this has on a text. • When you discuss a text's graphology you describe and analyse features like the **typeface**, the **positioning** of text on a page and the relationships between **text** and **images**.
Discourse	• **Discourse** is an **extended** piece of spoken or written language, made up of more than one **utterance** (in spoken language), or more than one **sentence** (in written language).

Language Frameworks

Discourse has a Structure

The way language is organised is called its **discourse structure**. You need to look out for different features, depending on whether the discourse is written or spoken.

1) In **written discourse**, look at how a text is **put together**. It may have an **opening** section which leads the reader into the text. The following sections may develop a **theme or argument**. The final section may make some kind of **conclusion**.

2) In **spoken discourse** the structure can be less organised. For example, **conversations** are often **unpredictable** and speakers often **digress** (go off the subject). This is because conversations are usually **spontaneous**.

3) Even spontaneous conversation has some structure, though.

There'll often be an **opening sequence**, e.g.

> Speaker 1: *Hi, how you doing?*
> Speaker 2: *Fine thanks. How about you?*

This is often followed by **turn-taking** as the speakers talk about a topic (or topics). There's often a **closing sequence** too, e.g.

> Speaker 1: *Well, nice seeing you...*
> Speaker 2: *You too.*
> Speaker 1: *Catch you later.*

4) You can also look at how the discourse **fits together** — **cohesion**. There are **two types** of cohesion — **lexical** and **grammatical**. One example of grammatical cohesion is using **adverbs** like *furthermore* and *similarly* at the beginning of a sentence or paragraph to link it to the previous one. Lexical cohesion is when the words in the discourse **relate** to each other throughout, e.g.

> There was no sign of **the car** — **her lift** was obviously stuck in **traffic**.
> Was it really worth it, just for a **ride** in a **Porsche**?

There are Three Main Steps to discourse analysis

1) The **first step** in **discourse analysis** is to think about **what kind** of discourse you are looking at. To do this you need to think about genre, register, audience, subject, purpose and mode.

2) The **next step** is to look at how each of the **language frameworks** contribute to the discourse. You might not need to use all of the language frameworks, or you might need to give more emphasis to one than another. It depends on the discourse.

3) And finally, don't forget to discuss **discourse structure** (how the text has been organised) and **cohesion** (the devices used to knit the text together).

Keith tried to look busy but his approach had been spotted.

Practice Questions

Q1 Give two examples of written discourse.
Q2 What is the difference between lexis and semantics?
Q3 What is phonology the study of?
Q4 Define discourse.
Q5 What is grammatical cohesion?

Discourse is brilliant — way better than those Science and Maths ones...

Soooo... your first two pages of AS English Language. They weren't so bad, were they? Didn't think so — but they are vital for your exam. It's really important to get into the habit of applying these frameworks to texts that you have to analyse. Think of them as guidelines that are there to help you organise your work. Aww, see? That's nice.

Introduction to Grammar

Grammar is one of the most important language frameworks — it covers everything from bits of words to entire sentences.

Grammar controls how **Language** is **Constructed**

1) Grammar is the set of **structural rules** that controls the way language works.

2) There are **three aspects** of grammar that you need to focus on — word classes, syntax and morphology.

3) **Word classes** define the **roles** that each word can play in a sentence. **Syntax** is the set of **rules** that control where each word class can appear in a sentence. **Morphology** describes the **construction** of individual words.

There are **Eight Main Word Classes**

Words are **categorised** by the **function** they have in a sentence.
There are eight main **word classes** — also called **parts of speech**.

Word Class	Function	Example
Nouns	'naming' words	*London, book, romance*
Adjectives	describe nouns (and sometimes pronouns)	*large, sunny, featureless*
Verbs	'doing' words	*jump, read, return*
Adverbs	describe verbs (and sometimes adjectives and other adverbs too)	*steadily, incredibly, sadly*
Pronouns	take the place of nouns	*you, they, him, me, it*
Conjunctions	'connecting' words	*and, or, but, because*
Prepositions	define relationships between words in terms of time, space and direction	*before, underneath, through*
Determiners	give specific kinds of information about a noun (e.g. quantity or possession)	*a, the, two, his, few, those*

Word classes are **Controlled** by **Rules**

Word classes can take **different positions** in a sentence, but there are **grammatical rules** about how they work with each other (**syntax**). In the following sentence you can see all the word classes working together:

She	saw	the	new	manager	and	his	assistant
pronoun	verb	determiner	adjective	noun	conjunction	determiner	noun

at	the	store	yesterday.
preposition	determiner	noun	adverb

1) People **instinctively** know the rules for connecting words together. For example, you know that words in this order — *doctor she the yesterday saw* — are wrong, and you can **rearrange** them into something that makes sense straight away — *she saw the doctor yesterday*.

2) You also intuitively know **less obvious rules** about word order — you'd always say *the big brown bear* rather than *the brown big bear*, because you know that adjectives of size **come before** those of colour.

3) Sometimes there are **fewer restrictions** — some sentences mean the same thing wherever a word is placed, particularly with **adverbs**, e.g. *I completely disagree* or *I disagree completely*.

4) Sometimes the **meaning** of a sentence changes depending on the position of a word:
   *He **quickly** told me to leave* (he said it fast)   **or**   *He told me to leave **quickly*** (he wanted me to leave fast)

Grammatical rules **Affect Word Formation**

Grammar affects word formation (morphology) because extra bits have to be added to words to **change** things like number or tense. The extra bits are called **inflections**. Here are a couple of examples.

- *-s* is added to *cup* to change a **singular** noun into a **plural** — *cups* (p.6).

- *-ed* is added to *remember* to change the **present** tense verb into the **past** tense *remembered* (p.8).

Introduction to Grammar

Grammar choices can Influence the reader or listener

You can influence your **audience** in different ways by **changing** the **grammar** of a word or sentence.

Tense

1) Events that happened in the past are usually described in the past tense. Sometimes however, in both spoken and written discourse, past events are described using **present tense forms**.

> • So she **went** up to the customer and **gave** him a good telling off.　　← past tense
> • So she **goes** up to the customer and **gives** him a good telling off.　　← present tense

2) The first example sentence is in the past tense. There is a clear sense that some **time has passed** since the event actually happened. In the second, although the action happened in the past, the present tense creates a more **immediate** and **dramatic** impact. You'll see this technique used a lot in **newspaper headlines**:

> New evidence casts doubt on verdict 　　 Pop star admits to private hell 　　 Cop raid closes nightclub

Plurals

1) As well as telling you that there's more than one of something, plurals can **increase** the scale of a **scene**.

> • There was a **mass** of fans outside the hotel.　　← singular
> • There were **masses** of fans outside the hotel.　　← plural

2) Using the singular form *mass* creates the impression of a **specific** body of people. Adding the **-es inflection** to form the plural *masses* creates the image of a **big crowd** of people across a **wider area**.

Adjectives

1) Adjectives are a great way to **influence** your **audience** — compare the following two examples:

> • If you're looking for the holiday of a lifetime, simply treat yourself to a **great** resort in Sri Lanka. Relax in **fine** accommodation.　　← simple adjectives
> • Looking for the holiday of a lifetime? Simply treat yourself to the **greatest** resort in Sri Lanka. Relax in the **finest** accommodation.　　← superlative adjectives

2) These are similar **advertising discourses**, but the second example is much more **persuasive** than the first. The writer uses **superlative** adjectives (see p.7) (*greatest* and *finest*) rather than the simple adjectives in the first example (*great* and *fine*).

3) There are some **other grammatical features** that influence the reader in these examples.

- The second example begins with a **question**. This makes the reader feel **involved immediately**.
- The first example uses the **indefinite article** *a* before the adjective *great*, but the second uses the **definite article** *the* before *greatest* (see p. 10). This makes the reference very **specific** in the second example (it is **the** greatest resort), but the first could be referring to any one of **several** resorts.

Practice Questions

Q1　In the following sentence, identify each word according to word class:

> *It was a cold winter and the Russian soldiers suffered terribly.*

Q2　Define the term syntax.

Q3　Why does this sentence sound awkward?

> *My blue old raincoat is now in tatters.*

What rule about word order can you deduce from this?

If you don't take precautions, you could get a nasty inflection...

I know — grammar's got a reputation for being a bit stale and boring. But if you don't understand the way language works and how everything is put together, and how important this is in discourse, then you can wave your analysis bye-bye. Luckily for you, we're about to get into a bit more detail, so get ready to become a world-class word-classer...

Nouns and Adjectives

Nouns are often called naming words, but at AS, it's all a bit more complicated than that. Nouns do give the names of places, people and things — but they can also refer to groups, states, emotions and more.

Nouns can be **Divided** into **Categories**

There are different **types** of nouns. They can refer to unique **people** or **places** (**proper nouns**), or identify more general **objects**, **states** or **groups** (**common nouns**). See below for some examples.

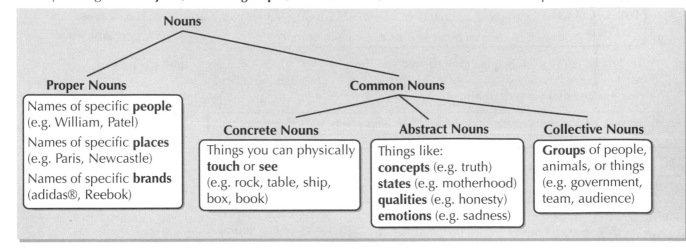

Nouns can be either **Singular** or **Plural**

1) To form the **plural** of a noun you usually add an -s or -es so that you get, for example, *birds,* or *buses.*

2) Where a noun ends in a consonant and then -y, the -y is replaced with -ies e.g. *lady* ⟶ *ladies.*

3) Words that include an *f* like *knife* and *dwarf* often replace the *f* with -ves ⟶ *knives* and *dwarves.*

4) Other nouns form **irregular plurals**, different from the **standard** pattern, e.g.
woman ⟶ *women*   *foot* ⟶ *feet*   *mouse* ⟶ *mice*

5) There are some nouns that **don't change their form** at all, whether they are singular or plurals, e.g. *deer* and *sheep* stay the same even when you are referring to more than one.

Nouns can be classified as **Count Nouns** or **Mass Nouns**

1) **Count nouns** (a bit obviously) can be **counted** — like *brick*. You can have *one brick, two bricks, three bricks,* and so on. Nouns that form irregular plurals can be count nouns too — *one mouse, two mice,* etc.

2) **Mass nouns** can't be counted. Nouns like these **don't** have a **plural**, e.g. you talk about *information* rather than *informations.*

3) Some nouns can function as **both** count and mass nouns, depending on the **context**. For example, in the phrase *war is evil*, *war* is a **mass noun** — it refers to war in general. However, *war* becomes a **count noun** when you use a determiner — e.g. *the war is evil*. This time *war* refers to a **specific** war rather than war in general.

Nouns can be **Modified** to give **More Information**

Nouns **don't usually stand alone**. They're often accompanied by words that **modify** them or that tell you **more** about them. There are two types of modifier — **pre-modifiers** and **post-modifiers**.

- **Pre-modifiers** — these come **before** the noun, e.g. a sign that reads *Dangerous Animal*. The adjective *dangerous* premodifies *animal* and tells you something about it. You can also have **more than one** pre-modifier, e.g. *very dangerous animal* — *very* and *dangerous* are both pre-modifiers.

- **Post-modifiers** — these come after the noun, e.g. *Examination in progress*. The noun *examination* is post-modified by *in progress* — it tells the reader something about the examination.

In **noun phrases**, the noun is called the **head word** — the most important word of the phrase. The other words **modify** it.

determiner	pre-modifier	head	post-modifier
the	*largest*	*whale*	*in the world*

Nouns and Adjectives

Adjectives **Describe Nouns**

Adjectives are classified according to their **position** — **before** or **after** the noun.

1) **Attributive** adjectives are **pre-modifying**, e.g. *the **sudden** noise*, or *the **red** balloon*.

2) **Predicative** adjectives are **post-modifying**. They're usually **linked** to the noun they are modifying by a form of the verb *be*:

> **Examples of predicative adjectives**
>
> - *Revision is **brilliant*** — the adjective is **linked** to the noun by a form of the verb *be*.
> - *The food looked **amazing*** — although forms of *be* are the most common links, **other verbs** can link the adjective to the noun (e.g. *looked, seemed, felt*)

Adjectives also make **Comparisons**

Adjectives are **gradable** — they can show **how much** of a certain property a noun displays.

1) **Comparative adjectives** are formed by adding an *-er* **inflection**. For example, the simple adjective *long* becomes the comparative adjective *long**er***.

2) **Superlative adjectives** are formed by adding *-est*. For example, *long* becomes the superlative *long**est***.

Look back at p.5 to see the effects of gradable adjectives in the holiday advertisement texts. Gradable adjectives make you interpret the sentences and the type of accommodation they advertise differently:

fine accommodation	*finer* accommodation	*finest* accommodation
simple adjective	**comparative adjective**	**superlative adjective**

3) Some adjectives are **irregular**:

Adjective	Comparative	Superlative
good	→ better	→ best
bad	→ worse	→ worst
much	→ more	→ most
little	→ less	→ least

4) Some adjectives need *more* and *most* to form comparisons. For example, you can't say *significant**er*** or *significant**est***. You use ***more** significant* or ***most** significant* to make the comparison.

Practice Questions

Q1 In the following list of common nouns, identify three concrete, three abstract and three collective nouns:
> *love, table, purity, family, government, disgust, team, wall, sock*

Q2 Which of the following are count nouns and which are mass nouns?
> *house, isolation, monkey, furniture, rat, gratitude, hall, courage, jug*

Q3 Identify the determiner, pre-modifier, head word and post-modifier in the following noun phrase:
> *One fine morning in July*

Q4 Identify the attributive adjective and the predicative adjective in the following phrases:
> *The storm was terrible*   *The terrible storm*

<u>Be Here Noun — and other great language albums...</u>

Like 'Noun That's What I Call Music... 88'. Or 'Urban Hymns', by The Verb. Or... never mind. Remember that nouns don't just name specific objects like pencils or sheds — they can refer to states or emotions as well. Get that idea firmly wedged into your head, and then you can go back to making up amusing grammar-based band names. If you want to, obviously.

Verbs and Adverbs

Without verbs, everything in language would stand still. That's why they're sometimes called 'doing' words.

Verbs tell you exactly **What Happens**

The base form of a verb is called the **infinitive** — it normally follows 'to', e.g. to *be*, to *laugh*, or to *think*.
You can describe verbs in two ways:

1) **Main Verbs** (lexical verbs) identify the action of the sentence — e.g. *she **sings** like a hyena, he **gave** me his shoe*. The **verbs** *sing* and *gave* tell you the **action** which is taking place.

2) **Auxiliary Verbs** go **before** the main verb in a sentence. They give **extra information** about the main verb and can affect the **meaning** of the sentence. There are **two** types of auxiliary verb:

Primary auxiliaries
There are three primary auxiliaries
— *do, have,* and *be.*

- *I **do** like you*
- *I **am** leaving tomorrow*

Primary auxiliaries can also be **main verbs**:

- *I **have** a surprise for you*

Modal auxiliaries
Modal auxiliaries can **only** occur with reference to a main verb.
There are 9 modal auxiliary verbs:

can	*could*	*will*	*would*	*must*
may	*might*	*shall*	*should*	

- *I **can** play the drums*
- *I **must** do something* (modal auxiliary before primary main verb)

Verbs can **Change** their endings depending on who is **Doing the Action**

The **endings** of verbs can alter depending on **who** is doing the action — the **person**.

Person	Singular	Verb	Plural	Verb
First	I	play	We	play
Second	You	play	You	play
Third	She/He/It	play**s**	They	play

Only the verb in the third person singular changes its ending — you add an -s to get plays. *This rule applies to most of the verbs in English.*

Changes to the ends of words that affect the grammar of the sentence are called **inflections**.

Verbs can tell you **When** something happens

Verbs change depending on whether something is happening in the **past**, **present**, or **future**.

1) **Present tense** tells you about 'now' and uses the **base form** of the verb, e.g. *I write* or *they dance* — unless it's the third person singular (see above), when you need to add the *-s* **inflection**, e.g. *she/he/it talks*.

2) **Past tense** tells you about the past (obviously), e.g. *I danced yesterday*, or *He missed the bus*. For most verbs, you form the past tense by **adding -ed** on the end — another **inflection**.

3) **Future tense** — Some people say that there's no future tense in English. This is because there **isn't** anything specific (like *-s*, or *-ed*) that you can **add** to a verb to show that the action will happen in the future. The future is expressed in **other ways** — often by using **modal auxiliary** verbs like **will** or **shall**.
   e.g. *I **shall** see you tomorrow*   *I **will** pick you up at eight*

4) You can also use the **present tense** to talk about **future events** — e.g. *Rachel is **playing** hockey on Saturday*.

Verbs **Don't** always change in the **Same Way**

1) Most verbs are **regular** — they follow the same patterns outlined above.

2) Some verbs are **irregular** — they don't change like you'd expect, e.g. *I drink* becomes *I **drank**, not I **drinked***. Other verbs with irregular past tenses include ***run**, **sing**, **write***, and ***speak***.

3) The verb *be* is very irregular — the forms it can take are the infinitive *to be*, plus *am, are, is, was,* and *were*. It changes according to **person** (first, second or third), and **singular / plural**, as well as **tense**, more than any other.

Verbs and Adverbs

Verbs can create an Active or Passive voice

Sentences that involve an **action** can focus on either the **subject** or the **object**.

Active Voice

The **active voice** is when the subject is the focus and **performs** the action described by the verb, e.g:

- *Ahmed kicked the ball.*

The subject, *Ahmed*, acts **directly** upon the object — *the ball*. The object **receives** the action of the verb.

Passive Voice

The **passive voice** is less direct. It focuses on the object. The **order changes** so that the object comes first, followed by the subject, e.g:

- *The ball was kicked by Ahmed.*

The passive voice makes sentences seem more **formal**.

Verbs can change depending on the Aspect

Aspect shows whether the action described by the verb has **finished**, or is still **being performed**.

PROGRESSIVE ASPECT

1) The **progressive** (or **continuous**) aspect refers to actions that don't have a definite end.

2) It's made up of one of the auxiliary forms of *be* and the **present participle** of a verb, which is the **base form** + *-ing*.

3) For example, in the sentence *They are doing well*, *are* is an auxiliary form of *be* and *doing* is the present participle of *do*.

PERFECT ASPECT

1) The **perfect aspect** tells you about an action that have a definite end.

2) It's made up of one of the present forms of *have* (has/have) and the past tense form of the verb, e.g. *They have bought a car.*

3) The **past perfect** aspect is formed in the same way but with the past tense of *have* (had), e.g. *I had missed it.*

Adverbs are used to Modify verbs

Adverbs are mostly used to modify verbs but they can modify nouns and adjectives too. Most people recognise adverbs as '**-ly** words' but many have different endings. Here are a **few ways** that adverbs **modify meaning**:

- Adverbs of **manner** — how something is done — e.g. *He talks incessantly*.
- Adverbs of **place** — where something is happening — e.g. *The book is here*.
- Adverbs of **time** — when something is happening — e.g. *The exam is tomorrow*.
- Adverbs of **duration** — how long something happens for — e.g. *The bridge is temporarily out of bounds*.
- Adverbs of **frequency** — how often something takes place — e.g. *Mandy visits sometimes*.
- Adverbs of **degree** — the extent to which something is done — e.g. *We completely understand*.

Some adverbs **express feelings** or opinions — *Hopefully, we'll find out where the garage is.*

Adverbs can also **link** sentences together — *The man was a great athlete. However, he didn't have a clue about adverbs.*

Practice Questions

Q1 Identify the verbs in the following sentence and state what tense they are written in.
Aiden went to see his friend Sally, but she was not in.

Q2 Identify one primary auxiliary verb, one modal auxiliary verb and one progressive verb in the following sentence.
Mohammed is going into town after college and therefore will be home late.

Q3 Rewrite this sentence in the active voice.
The glass was dropped by the waitress.

Q4 Identify two adverbs in the following sentences and explain their function.
Frankly, I disagree. Furthermore, I think your manner is despicable.

A'spect your head's still spinning after that lot — time for a lie down...

Verbs are pretty tricky customers, so it's vital that you get all this information inside that head of yours. The best way to practise this stuff is to apply it to real life — you'll notice verbs and adverbs popping up all over the place fairly frequently. Like in that last sentence — four main verbs, one modal auxiliary (in you'll), and two adverbs. I spoil you, I know.

Pronouns and Determiners

Pronouns and determiners are both related to nouns, but you never see them in the same place at the same time. They're like Bruce Wayne and Batman — and only a teensy bit less exciting.

Pronouns **Take** the **Place** of **Nouns**

Pronouns are a **sub-class** of **nouns**. They can identify subjects and objects, just like nouns do.

1) **Personal** pronouns can replace people or things who are the **subject** of a sentence. They're classified in terms of **person** and are either **singular** or **plural**:

	Singular	Plural
First Person	I	we
Second Person	you	you
Third Person	he, she, it	they

e.g. *Sarah thanked Sanjay*
↓
She *thanked Sanjay*
(3rd person singular subject pronoun)

2) Pronouns can also be used to replace the person or thing who is the **object** of the sentence:

	Singular	Plural
First Person	me	us
Second Person	you	you
Third Person	him, her, it	them

e.g. *Graham thanked Adam*
↓
*Graham thanked **him***
(3rd person singular object pronoun)

Pronouns are used in **Other Ways** too

1) **Interrogative** pronouns are used to **ask questions**. They are *which, what, who, and whose*. As with other pronouns, they help you **simplify** your sentences by **replacing nouns**, e.g:

- *Give me the name of **the person** you're looking for* ⟶ **Who** *are you looking for?*
- *Tell me **the thing** you are going to do* ⟶ **What** *are you going to do?*

2) These aren't the only words you use at the start of questions. *Why, where, how* and *when* are also interrogatives, but they are **adverbs**. Interrogative pronouns and adverbs are usually **classed together** as *wh-words*.

3) **Demonstrative** pronouns like *this, that, these* and *those* can **replace** people and things in a sentence where there's some **shared understanding** of what's being referred to, for example:

- If you're in the kitchen, you might ask *is this my coffee?* — only people who are also in the kitchen will be able to tell you.

- You use different demonstratives depending on the **distance** of the object from the speaker — *this* and *these* are objects **near** the speaker. You use *that* or *those* for objects **further away**.

Determiners show what the noun is **Referring To**

There are several determiners, which all **go before** the noun and show what it's referring to.

1) The **definite article** *the* and the **indefinite article** *a* refer to nouns. The definite article indicates something **specific**. The indefinite article indicates something more **general**, for example:

*Is that **the** frog?* (we are looking for, specifically) **or** *Is that **a** frog?* (or is it a toad?)

2) **Numerals** such as *one, two,* and *three* (cardinal numbers) and *first, second* etc. (ordinal numbers) are determiners.

3) **Possessive pronouns** like *my, your, his, her, its, our,* and *their* are determiners. They're used before a noun to show **possession** e.g. *my* car, *his* friend, *their* problem.

4) **Quantifiers** are determiners that show **quantity**, like *few, many* and *enough*.

5) **Demonstrative adjectives**, e.g. *this, that, these,* and *those* are also determiners. They **look the same** as demonstrative pronouns but there is a **significant difference** between them. They refer to specific objects or people that the participants are close to, rather than replacing them like pronouns do:

*I like **those*** **or** *I like **those** shoes*
*(those **replaces** the noun — pronoun)* *(those **precedes** the noun — adjective / determiner)*

Prepositions and Conjunctions

Prepositions show Relationships between things

Prepositions show the **relationship** between things in terms of **space**, **time** or **direction**. The preposition usually goes before the determiner and noun.

- *The books are **underneath** the bed* (spatial)
- *She left **before** the end* (time)
- *He moved **towards** the door* (directional)

Sometimes there's no determiner e.g. ⟹
- *See you **at** breaktime.*
- *We'll talk more about it **on** Friday.*

Conjunctions are Linking Words

There are **two types** of conjunction — **coordinating** conjunctions and **subordinating** conjunctions.

1) **Coordinating conjunctions** are words like *and*, *but*, and *or*. They **connect** single words or longer units of language (phrases and clauses) that have **equal status**:

| *Robert **and** Bethany* | *A white shirt **or** a pink shirt* | *He kissed her on the cheek **and** she ran away* |

The **coordinating conjunction** *and* connects the two names — neither is given more importance.

The **coordinating conjunction** *or* links **two phrases**.

The coordinating conjunction *and* links two **equal statements**.

2) **Subordinating conjunctions** are words like *since, although, because, unless, whether* and *whereas*. They link a main clause to one that's **less important** to the subject of the sentence:

*Some people find Maths really difficult, **whereas** others find it easy.*

> More about clauses on p12-13.

The main clause is *Some people find Maths really difficult*. This is the subject of the sentence. The **subordinating conjunction** *whereas* introduces a less important clause *others find it easy*.

Other subordinating conjunctions give **different meanings**.
Some, like *after, before* and *until* are to do with **time**. Others like *where* and *wherever* are about **place**.

1) Conjunctions are an important **cohesive device** — they help a discourse to flow smoothly.

2) A discourse **without** conjunctions seems very **disjointed** — e.g. *Last night I went out. I bumped into my friend Hayley. We talked for a while. She had to leave early. She was babysitting for her auntie.*

3) If you add **conjunctions**, the discourse is much more **fluent** — e.g. *Last night I went out **and** I bumped into my friend Hayley. We talked for a while **but** she had to leave early **because** she was babysitting for her auntie.*

Practice Questions

Q1 Identify three personal pronouns in the following sentence.
I doubt whether you will like it.

Q2 Identify an interrogative pronoun and a demonstrative pronoun in the following sentence.
Where are you going with that?

Q3 Identify the determiners in the following sentence:
There were twenty fish in my pond this year.

Q4 Find a coordinating conjunction and a subordinating conjunction in the following sentence.
The teacher and her pupils fled the building because it was on fire.

Just when you thought classes were over, it's time for two more terms...

But at least they're short. Like gnomes. Nouns, verbs, adjectives and adverbs are known as open-class or lexical words. Pronouns, determiners, conjunctions and prepositions are known as closed-class or grammatical words. The lexical words are the content of a sentence, and the grammatical words perform functions that link them all together. Ah, unrivalled joy...

Phrases and Clauses

When you're analysing word classes, you need to focus on the function of individual words. The next level of analysis after this is to look at larger units of language like phrases and clauses. Onwards and upwards, and all that...

Phrases are **Units** of **Language** that have a **Head Word**

Phrases are units of language built around a **head word** that identifies the type of phrase, e.g. in the noun phrase *the empty house*, the noun *house* is the head word. Basic sentences are created from a combination of phrases.

1) The simplest noun phrase (NP) possible is just a **noun itself**.
   It can be accompanied by a **pre-modifier**, a **post-modifier**, or both.

Pre-modifiers come before the noun. They're often a determiner, followed by an adjective.	pre-modifiers		head word	post-modifiers		Post-modifiers come after the noun.
	determiner	adjective	noun	preposition	noun	
	the	*new*	*mayor*	*of*	*Bradford*	

2) A very simple verb phrase (VP) has **one verb**, but you can also make up a verb phrase from the head word (a main verb) and one or more **auxiliary** verbs.

auxiliary	auxiliary	head word
should	*have*	*passed*

3) For example — the **noun phrases** and **verb phrases** are underlined in the following sentences:
   <u>The wealthy woman</u> <u>has been</u> to <u>London</u> many <u>times</u>. Now <u>she</u> <u>is planning</u> <u>a trip to Paris</u>.

A **Clause** is a **Unit** of a **Sentence**

1) Sentences are made up of **clauses** — the **simplest meaningful units** of the sentence.

2) A **sentence** can be made up of **one clause** — e.g. *Katherine likes going walking*.

3) Or it can be made up of **more than one** clause. When there's more than one clause in a sentence, the clauses are separated by **conjunctions** — e.g. *Katherine likes going walking **but** she doesn't like running*.

4) **Clauses** can be made up of a **subject**, **verb**, **object**, **complement** and **adverbial**.

5) The verb, complements and adverbials of a clause or sentence are sometimes also called the **predicate**. The term 'predicate' refers to any part of the clause that is **not the subject**, but that **modifies** it in some way. The verb is sometimes referred to as the **predicator**.

E.g. ***Harry chased the squirrel***

The **subject** is the person or thing that **does something** in the clause. *Harry* is the subject because he's **doing** the chasing. The subject can also be *it*, as in *it is snowing*, or *it is eight o'clock*.

The **verb** (or verb phrase) tells you what the subject is doing. Here the subject *Harry* is followed by the verb *chased*.

The **object receives** the **action**. In this clause *the squirrel* is the object because it's having the action done to it — it's being chased by the subject.

A **complement** gives more **information about** the **subject** or **object**. It **completes** the **meaning** of the sentence it appears in, for example:

- In *Harry is a great guitarist*, the noun phrase (NP) *Harry* is the subject. The second NP in the sentence, *a great guitarist* is a subject complement. It **completes** the meaning of the sentence by giving information about the subject.

- In *Harry found the film appalling*, *Harry* is still the subject. But the adjective *appalling* refers to *the film*, which is the object, so *appalling* is the **object complement**.

An **adverbial** is a word or group of words that **refer back to the verb**. The simplest adverbial is just an adverb e.g. *Harry kicked the ball **quickly***. In *Harry is playing on Sunday*, the adverbial is *on Sunday* as it relates to the specific time that Harry will play. Adverbials usually describe **time**, **place** or **manner**.

Phrases and Clauses

There are **Seven** Common Types of **Clause**

These are created by **different combinations** of subject (**S**), verb (**V**), object (**O**), complement (**C**) and adverbial (**A**):

S + V	Harry + played
S + V + O	Harry + played + a game
S + V + C	Harry + was + great
S + V + A	Harry + played + on Tuesday
S + V + O + O	Harry + gave + him + a drink
S + V + O + C	Harry + thought + his performance + disappointing
S + V + O + A	Harry + passed + the ball + quickly

Harry + fluorescent trunks + chest wig = one hot look.

Clauses are defined by **Status**

The **status** of a clause depends on its **constituents** and whether it can **stand alone** as a meaningful unit of language.

1) **Main clauses** — (**independent clauses**) can stand alone and still make sense:

> *Harry played.*

2) **Coordinate clauses** — occur in sentences where there are **two or more** independent clauses.
- They're joined together by a **coordinating conjunction** like *and* or *but*. For example:

> *The band played for two hours **but** I had to leave early.*

- The clauses could **stand alone** and still **make sense** — *The band played for two hours. I had to leave early.*

3) **Subordinate clauses** — can't stand alone. They have to be with a **main clause**.
- A subordinate clause gives **extra information** about the main clause.
- In most cases, a subordinate clause is led by a **subordinating conjunction** (like *since, although, because, unless, if, whether, while, whereas* etc.). This links it to the main clause. For example:

main clause ⟹ *Will you pop in to see me **while** you're here tomorrow?* ⟸ subordinate clause (the clause can't stand alone in a meaningful way)

subordinating conjunction

4) **Combining clauses** — you can combine coordinate and subordinate clauses in the same sentence:

> *He went his way **and** she went hers **because** they did not see eye to eye.*

coordinate clause   coordinating conjunction   coordinate clause   subordinating conjunction   subordinate clause

Practice Questions

Q1 Identify the head word, pre-modifiers and post-modifiers (where applicable) in the following noun phrases:
the gold bracelet   *a cold, frosty morning in spring*   *fish and chips from the shop*

Q2 Identify verb phrases in the following clauses:
Joshua should tell her   *You should have seen it*   *I will be leaving early tomorrow*

Q3 Which is the main clause and which is the subordinate clause in the following sentence?
It was still dark when the travellers rose from their slumbers.

Don't let all this stuff get on top of you... it'd be dead clause-trophobic...

To get the hang of how these phrases and clauses work, practise identifying them — have a look at some articles or listen to the news and see if you can work out how the sentences all fit together. Refer back to these pages if you need to, and just keep going until it's a piece of cake. Mmm cake... Almost as much of a treat as learning about clauses, but not quite.

Sentences

So far you've seen how word classes, phrases and clauses fit together. Now for the big surprise. It turns out that they're all building blocks in sentences — the largest grammatical units. Well who'd have thought it...

Sentences can be anything from very **Simple** to really **Complex**

There are **five** types of sentence — **minor**, **simple**, **compound**, **complex** and **compound-complex**.

1) **Minor sentences** are complete and meaningful statements that **don't have** a subject and verb combination. Lots of everyday sayings are minor sentences, e.g. *Be quiet. Goodbye. Sounds good.*

2) A **simple sentence** must have a **subject** and a **verb**. It should express a **complete thought**, e.g. *The snow falls.* *Snow* is the **subject**, *falls* is the **verb**.

3) A **compound sentence** is an independent clause linked to another independent clause by a **coordinating conjunction**. Either one could be a main clause in a different sentence.

independent clause ➡ *I went to Manchester **and** I went to Liverpool.* ⬅ independent clause

coordinating conjunction

Upset the grammar sheriff — get a really long sentence.

4) A **complex sentence** consists of a main clause and a subordinate clause (or subordinating clauses). A **subordinating conjunction** connects the clauses together:

main clause ➡ *The workers left the building **when** they heard.* ⬅ subordinate clause

subordinating conjunction

5) A **compound-complex sentence** is made up of at least two **coordinate clauses** connected by a **coordinating conjunction**, and **at least one** subordinate clause.

*Some of the children went home early **but** the others remained **because** they had no transport.*

first coordinate clause — coordinating conjunction — second coordinate clause — subordinating conjunction — subordinate clause

The **Structure** of **Sentences** tells you about the **Target Audience**

1) The length and complexity of sentences can be varied according to the **content** and **audience** of a text.

2) A good example of contrasting sentence structures is the difference between **broadsheet** and **tabloid** newspapers.

BROADSHEET NEWSPAPER

The scientific community is under the microscope as it nears hybrid embryo creation.
(Complex sentence — main clause + subordinate clause)

This is a serious ethical issue since it questions the very nature of what it is to be human.
(Complex sentence — main clause + subordinate clause)

The intention to find new ways of treating hitherto untreatable illnesses is no doubt laudable but the cost to human life will be incalculable as live embryos will be destroyed after fourteen days.
(Compound-complex sentence — main clause + main clause + subordinate clause)

TABLOID NEWSPAPER

Mad scientists are on the verge of creating monsters.
(Simple sentence)

They will take the sperm and eggs of humans and animals and mix them up.
(Compound sentence — coordinate clause + coordinate clause)

Living embryos will be trashed after fourteen days.
(Simple sentence)

3) The writers create a different **mood** and **tone** depending on the types of sentences they use. They're intended to appeal to different **audiences**.

4) The first example is more complex — it has a **measured** and **balanced** feel to it. The second, relatively simple set of sentences is more **emotive** and **subjective**:

Sentences

You can **Classify Sentences** by their **Function**

Sentences have **four** functions.

1) DECLARATIVES

- **Declarative** sentences are statements that **give information**, e.g. ⟶

> *This summer was the hottest on record.*
> *I don't like cheese.*

2) IMPERATIVES

- **Imperative** sentences **give orders**, **instructions**, **advice** and **directions**.
- They **start** with a **main verb** and **don't** have a **subject**, e.g. ⟶

> **Go** *left and it's first on your right.*
> **Answer** *one question from each section.*

3) INTERROGATIVES

Interrogative sentences ask **questions**.

- Some questions are formed by **inverting** (swapping round) the **verb** and the **subject** of a sentence.

E.g. | **You are coming** out tonight. | ⟶ | **Are you coming** out tonight? |

Subject **Verb** **Main verb**   **Verb** **Subject** **Main verb**

- Interrogatives can start with **wh- words**, e.g. ⟶

> **Wh**ere are you going?
> **Wh**en will you be back?

- They can also be added to the **end of a statement**. These are called **tag questions**, e.g. ⟶

> *It's cold, **isn't it**?*
> *She said she was on her way, **didn't she**?*

- In **spoken discourse** you can turn **declarative statements** into questions using **stress** and **intonation**. This is called a **rising inflection**, e.g. ⟶

> *He will get better?*

4) EXCLAMATIVES

- **Exclamative** sentences have an **expressive function** — they convey the force of a statement, and end with an **exclamation mark**, e.g. ⟶

> *I will not do this any more!*
> *That was fantastic!*

Practice Questions

Q1 Identify whether the following sentences are minor or simple:
Good afternoon   *the doctor is here*   *the band was late*   *your turn*

Q2 Identify the coordinate clauses and the coordinating conjunction in this compound sentence:
Ravina is going to Delhi but I will stay in Calcutta.

Q3 Identify the main clause, the subordinate clause and the subordinating conjunction in this complex sentence:
I will stay in bed today because I'm not feeling very well.

Q4 In this compound-complex sentence, identify two coordinate clauses and one subordinate clause:
The band played brilliantly and the crowd screamed for more until the lights went out.

Minor sentences — great if you're down 'pit, rubbish if you're in an exam...

Brilliant. That was sentences. Learn this stuff and you'll be OK. It's very important because sentence structure can help identify a target audience. It might seem tedious, but you need to do it, because knowing all this syntax malarkey is useful. Ah, grammar — the most fun you can have in an empty room with no windows, lights, friends or board games.

Lexis

Not to be confused with the luxury Japanese car firm, lexis is just a fancy word for words. If you're thinking that words is a perfectly good word for words, then you'll be eating your words after you've read these words. No word of a lie.

Lexis means Words

1) **Lexis** is the linguistic term for **vocabulary** — the words of a language.

2) When you're **analysing language**, you'll start by looking at the lexis.

3) It's divided into **word classes** — also called the **parts of speech** (see p.4), e.g. nouns, verbs, adjectives.

4) Lexis can also be analysed in chunks or phrases, known as **lexical phrases**. These are well-known groups of words like *on the other hand* and *once upon a time*. There are hundreds of these phrases and they're used all the time.

English has been Influenced by Other Languages

1) A lot of the most frequently used words in the English vocabulary come from **Old English**. They're mostly **everyday** words like *that, house, on, be, bread*.

2) English developed from Old English with lots of borrowings from **French** and **Latin**.

3) This is one of the reasons why English has lots of **synonyms** (different words for the same thing, see p.19) — some are from one language, some from another.

4) Words with **Latin** origins tend to feel more **formal** than Old English ones — e.g. *chew* comes from Old English, *masticate* comes from Latin.

English is always Changing

1) English is still influenced by other languages. Words that are **borrowed** from other languages are called **loan words** — e.g. *shampoo* from Hindi, *bluff* from Dutch, *schmooze* from Yiddish. They become part of English through contact with other cultures.

2) Words also enter the language through advances in **science** and **technology**, which creates the need for **new words** (**neologisms**) — e.g. *email, genome*.

3) Once a word has entered the language, it can become part of **everyday English** in different ways:

Adding an affix

1) **Suffixes** are put **after** the root or stem of a word. These can alter the **meaning** of the word they're attached to and change its **word class**.

2) **Common** English suffixes are *–tion*, *-ness*, *-ish* and *–able*.

3) When nouns from other languages become part of **everyday English**, the plural is made by adding an *-s*. For example, the German word *Kindergärten* (meaning *more than one Kindergarten*) becomes *kindergartens* in English.

4) **Prefixes** are put **before** the root or stem of a word. They alter the meaning of the word, often **reversing** the original meaning.

5) Common English **prefixes** include *multi-*, *dis-*, *trans-* and *sub-*.

Conversion

1) This is where the **word classes** of existing words are **altered**.

2) For example — *gift* can be a **noun** (*the gift*), but it can also be used as a **verb** (*to gift*).

3) *Empty* is an **adjective**, but it can also be converted to a **verb** (*to empty*).

Creating compound words

1) **Compound words** are created by **joining** two or more words together.

2) For example, *rainbow* joins *rain* and *bow*.

3) The separate words are combined to create a **new meaning**, which is **different** to the meanings of the original words — e.g. *laptop* specifically refers to a computer you could rest on your knees.

Lexis

The **Lexis** people use depends on the **Situation**

Lexis has different **levels** of **formality**.

1) **Informal lexis** is relaxed, familiar and conversational.

2) It's **colloquial** and often **non-standard**, so it will contain **dialect** words and **slang** (see p.32-33 and p.38-39) — e.g. you might describe someone as being *tapped* or a *loony*.

3) It tends to be **smaller** than **formal lexis** and contain more **monosyllabic** words (see p.22) like *nice* and *grub*.

4) It contains lots of **abbreviations** like *can't*, *you'll* and *would've*.

5) Informal lexis for **ordinary** things often has **Old English** roots — e.g. *house*, *home*.

---

1) **Formal lexis** is more serious and impersonal.

2) It tends to be made up of **Standard English** words, so it's unlikely to contain **dialect** words or **slang**, e.g. someone might be described as *mentally ill* or *not in possession of their faculties*.

3) It's bigger and more complex than informal lexis, so there are more **polysyllabic** words (see p.22) like *enjoyable* and *comestibles*.

4) Words are less likely to be **abbreviated** — e.g. *do not* will be used rather than *don't*.

5) Formal lexis often has **Latinate** roots (it comes from Latin) — e.g. *residence*, *habitation*.

The **Lexis** of **Written** and **Spoken** English is very different

1) As a general rule, **written** language is **more formal** than **spoken** language.

2) The most **informal** language is found in **speech** between friends and family. The most **formal** language is found in **writing** between people who don't know each other — e.g. essays, business letters and broadsheet newspapers.

3) One of the main reasons for this is because **speech** tends to be **spontaneous**, so the lexis is **smaller** and there's lots of **self-correction** — speakers notice their own errors and correct them in mid-sentence.

4) Speech also tends to contain lots of **abbreviations**, like *shan't* and *gonna*. This is even the case with **planned speech**, which can sound strange and stilted if the speaker doesn't abbreviate some words.

5) However, there are situations where **speech** is more **formal** than **writing**. This is especially the case when it's **planned** — e.g. a politician's speech, or in a formal situation like a job interview.

6) Likewise, there are situations where **written language** is informal, e.g. an email between friends.

Practice Questions

Q1 What is lexis?

Q1 Outline how English has been influenced by other languages.

Q3 What is conversion?

Q4 Outline two differences between informal and formal language.

Essay Question

Q1 Outline how English has developed through the influence of different languages, and how it continues to change.

Lexis a nice name — short for Alex you know...

I've got that thing now where I've read the word 'word' so many times that it's started to look ridiculous. Word word word word word. It looks a bit gross somehow, like 'worm'. If this happens to you in the exam you may be forced to replace it with a substitute until the affliction wears off — something neutral like 'gentleman' or 'rice' would probably be best...

Semantics

Another hoity-toity, highfalutin, la-di-da bit of linguistic terminology here, but it's not as tricky as it looks. Semantics just means meaning, so if you've ever understood the meaning of a word then you shouldn't find the idea too difficult to grasp

Semantics is the Study of Meaning

Semantics looks at how the **meanings** of words are **constructed** and **interpreted**.

Denotation

1) Denotation is the **straightforward meaning** or **definition** of a word, which you'd find if you looked the word up in a **dictionary**.

2) For example, *red* is *'a primary colour that lies next to orange on the visible spectrum'*. *Cloud* is *'a mass of water or ice particles in the sky'*.

3) It's especially **important** for the denotation of words to be **clear** when people are giving **instructions** and **information**, e.g. in safety notices and scientific documents. Writers have to be careful to **avoid ambiguity** (see below), otherwise people might not understand the meaning properly.

Connotation

1) Connotation refers to the **associations** a word has, or the **emotions** raised by a word.

2) For example, *red* can be associated with love and passion, or with blood and danger. *Cloud* can be associated with fluffiness, blue skies and rainbows, or dreariness and sadness.

3) The **connotations** of words can be **ambiguous**, so **interpretations** can **vary** from person to person.

Implication

1) This is when the meaning is **suggested**, rather than being stated directly.

2) For example, if a child arrives home late from a party, their parents might say *'You're late!'*. Literally, all they're saying is that the child was expected home earlier. But the **implication** behind the words is *'You're in trouble — explain why you're late'*.

Ambiguity

1) This is where a word, phrase or argument can be **understood** or **interpreted** in **more than one way**.

2) For example, *men can't bear children* could mean *men can't give birth to children*, or *men hate children*.

3) Sometimes this is **unintentional**, and a case of the writer not checking carefully. Sometimes it's done **deliberately** to raise questions in the readers' minds.

Structural Semantics is about the Relationships between Words

Structural semantics looks at the different ways that **words relate** to **each other** through **meaning**.

1) Semantic Fields

1) **Semantic fields** (also called **lexical fields**) are **groups** of words that are **connected** in **meaning**.

2) E.g. the words *classroom, teacher, assembly, lesson* and *homework* are all in the **semantic field** of 'school'. Although the **meaning** of each word is different, they're all part of the same **framework**.

3) The words (lexis) that make up the semantic field are known as **field-specific lexis**.

Here are some more examples of **semantic fields** and **field-specific lexis**...

Semantic field of **war**

artillery   bomb   naval
air force   gas   insurgence
combat   weapon

Semantic field of the **body**

hair   circulation
respire   skin   muscle
legs   cell   heart

Semantics

2) Synonyms

1) **Synonyms** are words that have **similar meanings**, e.g. *grub* and *comestibles* are synonyms for *food*.

2) Synonyms can have different **connotations**, so their meaning isn't identical, e.g. *grub* is informal and suggests that the food is quite plain, *comestibles* is more formal and old fashioned. Talking about someone's *children* has different connotations to talking about their *brats*.

3) Using a particular synonym over another can be a **regional variation** (see p.32), e.g. saying *bairn* instead of *child*, or *mardy* instead of *grumpy*.

4) You use different synonyms depending on the **situation**, e.g. in a formal letter you might write about *working*, but in informal speech you might talk about *slogging away*.

It seemed that Max thought 'girlfriend' was a synonym for 'foot rest'.

3) Antonyms

1) **Antonyms** are words with **opposite meanings**.

2) For example — *hot / cold, male / female, day / night, sweet / sour*.

3) Antonym **pairs** are often used together as **comparisons** — e.g. *I'm always tired during the **day** but I wake up at **night**,* or *you're blowing **hot** and **cold** with me.*

4) They tend to be quite **rigid**, so they don't necessarily work with **other synonyms** — e.g. you wouldn't say *hot / cool, male / feminine, day / evening*.

4) Hypernyms and Hyponyms

This can be a bit confusing at first, but bear with it because it becomes clearer once you've seen some examples:

1) Basically, a **hypernym** is a **general** word. A **hyponym** is **specific** word with a meaning that's **linked** to the hypernym.

2) For example, *school* is a **hypernym**. Words describing more **specific types** of school, such as *primary*, *secondary*, *grammar*, *comprehensive* are **hyponyms**.

3) Words can be **hypernyms** in one context and **hyponyms** in another, e.g. *fruit* is a **hyponym** of *food*, because it's a **specific type** of food. But it's also a **hypernym** for *melon*, because *melon* is a **specific type** of fruit.

Practice Questions

Q1 Which semantic fields could these words belong to — bed, wine, wicket?

Q2 Explain the difference between a synonym and an antonym.

Q3 Explain the difference between a hypernym and a hyponym.

Essay Question

Q1 Place the word **adult** into each of the categories on these pages, and explain how it fits there. E.g. its connotations, how it's ambiguous, which semantic fields it fits into, and some synonyms for it.

Relationships between words can be very meaningful...

Lots of technical words to get to grips with here, but it'll look really good if you can use some of them. All this hypernym / hyponym stuff can be a bit of a nightmare, but a handy way of remembering which is which is that hypernym is a longer word, for a bigger, more general thing. I'd like to say that antonyms had something to do with ants, but that would be a lie.

Semantics

You can get your meaning across literally (he's ugly), or you can inject a bit more interest with figurative language (he fell out of the ugly tree and hit every branch on the way down). This kind of language lets writers be a bit more creative.

Figurative Language isn't Literal

Figurative language (or **figures of speech**) **isn't** meant to be taken **literally**.
It's used to add colour to the language, and is classified into **different types**.

Figurative language	Explanation
Similes	1) Similes are comparisons that use the words 'like' or 'as'. 2) For example — *his hair was as white **as** snow, she can swim **like** a fish*. 3) The comparison is always stated **explicitly**, e.g. in the example above, she isn't **actually** a fish, she's just said to be **like** one.
Metaphors	1) Metaphors are comparisons that **don't** use 'like' or 'as'. 2) They describe a person, object or situation as if it actually were something else. 3) For example — *there was a **blanket** of snow on the ground*. The snow isn't actually a blanket, it's just **like** one. Because the comparison is **implicit** it's more **powerful** than a simile. 4) An **extended metaphor** is when the same metaphor is continued throughout a text to create a chain of images — e.g. if the *rain* is referred to as *tears*, then it's also referred to using other words relating to crying, e.g. *weeping, miserable*.
Personification	1) Personification is a type of **metaphor**, where an object or situation is given **human qualities**. 2) For example — *the wind wailed* creates the image of the wind having a mouth and being able to wail like a human.
Metonymy	1) Metonymy is using a **part** of something to describe the **whole** thing. 2) For example — the term *the crown* can be used to mean the *monarchy*, because one of the **attributes** of monarchs is that they wear a crown.
Oxymoron	1) An oxymoron brings two **conflicting ideas** together. 2) E.g. *bittersweet, living death, gentle tyrant*. 3) The separate meanings of both ideas are **combined** to create a new one, and to grab the reader's attention.

1) Some **figurative expressions** are used so much that they become part of **everyday language**, e.g. metaphorical expressions like *the **head** of the table*, and *the bank opened another **branch***.

2) These are known as **dead metaphors**, because they're not seen as comparisons any more, but just expressions in their own right.

3) When a figurative expression is **overused** then it can lose its impact or novelty value and become a **cliché**, e.g. the **similes** *as good as gold* and *as plain as the nose on your face*, and the **metaphors** *it's a piece of cake* and *I'm all ears*.

Jargon is the Specific Language people use at Work

There's loads more about **jargon** on p.40-41 and p.52, so this is just a quick glance at how it fits in with **semantics**.

1) Jargon is **specialist vocabulary** associated with a particular **occupation** or activity.

2) It tends to be more **formal** than everyday language, because it refers to **specific**, **technical** things.

3) This means it can be **difficult** for **non-specialists** to **understand**.

4) **Existing** words can take on **new meanings** within a specific environment.
For example, online advertisers might talk about *spiders* and *sticky*. These words have completely **different meanings** in the **context** of online advertising — a *spider* is a software program that automatically follows links, a *sticky* website is one that people stay on for longer than usual.

Semantics

Rhetorical Language *is designed to* Persuade

There are loads of **rhetorical devices** — here are some of the most common ones.

> **Three-part list**
> 1) This is where three elements are used in a list to give **emphasis** and build to a **climax**.
> 2) E.g. *blood, sweat and tears* is a list of three **nouns**, *he came, he saw, he conquered* lists three **verbs**.

> **Repetition**
> 1) **Repetition** is when a word or phrase is repeated for **emphasis**, for **emphasis**.
> 2) E.g. *it's not good enough, simply not good enough*.

> **Hyperbole**
> 1) Hyperbole means using **exaggeration** for **effect**, e.g. *I've told you a hundred times*.
> 2) The **media** use hyperbole to make stories seem more important, interesting or entertaining, e.g. describing a football referee's unfair decision as the *crime of the century*.

> **Rhetorical questions**
> 1) A rhetorical question doesn't require an **answer**, because it's phrased in a way that **assumes** the answer is obvious.
> 2) E.g. *how would you like to be in this position?*

Meaning *depends on* Context

1) Words can have different **meanings**, so readers have to rely on **context** to understand which meaning applies.
2) For example — the word *book*. When it's on its own, it's impossible to know whether it's the **noun** *book*, as in 'printed pages bound in a cover', or the verb *to book*, as in 'to book a hotel room'.
3) Writers sometimes take advantage of **double meanings** to suggest different ideas and make their work more layered. For example, in the sentence *Jonathan was trying*, *trying* could be a **verb**, suggesting that Jonathan was *trying* his hardest, or it could be an **adjective** suggesting that his personality was *trying* (irritating).

Practice Questions

Q1 Outline the difference between similes and metaphors.
Q2 What is the purpose of rhetorical language?
Q3 Why is hyperbole frequently used in the media?

Essay Question

Love's not Time's fool, though rosy lips and cheeks
Within his bending sickle's compass come:
Love alters not with his brief hours and weeks,
But bears it out even to the edge of doom.
If this be error and upon me proved,
I never writ, nor no man ever loved.

Sonnet CXVI, William Shakespeare, 1609

Q1 Analyse the use of figurative and rhetorical language in this extract.

These linguists seem to get up to sem very silly antics...

A good way to remember the difference between a simile and a metaphor is that a simile *says something is* similar *to something else, because it uses 'like' or 'as'. But if you really can't decide which one it is then you can just say that the language is figurative and leave it at that. What a great topic. And to top it all, simile looks a bit like smile — awww...*

Phonology

These seem like a couple of exciting pages. Look at them, all poised like a coiled spring to tell you everything you could ever wish to know about phonology — what the language sounds like. And I know one thing it sounds like — fun...

Phonetics and Phonology are Different

Phonetics

1) **Phonetics** is the study of how speech sounds are **made** and **received**.

2) It covers all **possible sounds** that the human vocal apparatus (vocal chords, tongue, lips, teeth, etc.) can make.

3) It focuses on **differences** in **articulation**, e.g. different accents.

Phonology

1) **Phonology** is the study of the **sound systems** of languages, in particular the **patterns** of sounds.

2) It focuses on **units** of sound, called **phonemes** (see below).

3) Unlike phonetics, in phonology you **don't** look at **differences** of **articulation**, e.g. if someone pronounces *stupid* as *shtupid*, the *s* and *sh* are still classed as the **same phoneme**, because the different pronunciation doesn't create a **different meaning**.

Phonemes are Units of Sound

1) The **smallest units** of **sound** are called **phonemes**. There are only about **44** phonemes in English, and combinations of them make up **all** the **possible** words and sounds in the language.

> This is the International Phonetic Alphabet (IPA). It's different to the normal alphabet because it's used for writing all the possible phonemes (sounds) that humans can make in any language. Slanting brackets are used to distinguish between phonemes.

2) For example, the word *cat* has **three** phonemes — /k/ (like the *c* in *coat*), /ae/ (like the *a* in *bat*) and /t/ (like the *t* in *toy*). By **changing** one of these phonemes (e.g. /f/ for /k/) you can create a new word, *fat*.

3) The 26 letters of the **alphabet** can express **all** the possible sounds in English, e.g. **pairs** of letters (**digraphs**) like *sh-* and *ch-* can be used to represent **single phonemes**.

4) The study of phonemes is divided into **vowel sounds** and **consonant sounds**.

Vowel Sounds

1) There are about **twenty vowel sounds** in English, even though there are only **five** vowels in the alphabet.

2) E.g. the vowel *a* has a different sound depending on the word in which it appears. In *ape* it sounds different to when it's in *sat*, *care* and *saw*.

3) Vowel sounds are usually in the **centre** of a **syllable**, e.g. b*a*g, c*oa*t.

4) When a vowel sound is spoken, the **vocal tract** is always **open** — the **airway** is clear and your **vocal chords** rub together to 'voice' the sound. Vowel sounds are made by **altering** the **shape** of the **mouth**. The way vowel sounds are **pronounced** **varies** in **different** regions. This is how people can tell the difference between accents (see p.32-33).

Consonant Sounds

1) The number of **consonant sounds** in English is close to the **actual** number of **consonants** in the **alphabet**.

2) Consonants are mostly found at the **edges** of **syllables**, e.g. *boy*s, *girl*s. Sometimes they can appear in **sequences** of three or four consonants **together**, e.g. *str*ing or twe*lfth*.

3) Unlike vowels, they're mostly articulated by **closing** the vocal organs.

4) Some consonants are formed by **vibration** of the vocal cords, e.g. /b/ and /n/. The amount of vibration depends on the **position** of the consonant within the word. At the end of the word, the consonant is less pronounced. Other consonants don't use the vocal cords at all, such as /p/ and /s/.

Words are made up of Syllables

Syllables are a word's **individual units** of pronunciation. They are normally **combinations** of consonants and vowels.

1) The **centre** of a syllable is a **vowel sound**, e.g. b*u*n, t*y*ke.

2) Syllables can have one or more **consonants before** the **vowel**, e.g. *b*e, *sl*ow.

3) Many syllables have one or more consonants **following** the **vowel**, e.g. a*nt*.

4) They can also have consonants before **and** following the vowel, e.g. *pla*y, *rea*d.

5) **Monosyllabic** words have **one syllable**, e.g. *plate*, *car*. **Polysyllabic words** have **more than one** syllable, e.g. *amazing* (*a-maz-ing*), *cryogenic* (*cry-o-gen-ic*).

Phonology

Words Sound Different when they're Connected

Words are often pronounced **differently** than you'd expect when you see them **written down**.
This is because spoken language **combines** and **runs** sounds together.

> **Elision** is when sounds are **left out**.
> 1) It happens especially in **rapid speech**, with words that have **clusters** of **consonants** or **syllables**.
> 2) For example, *library* is usually pronounced *libry*, and *everything* can become *evrythn*.

> **Assimilation** is when sounds that are next to each other become **more alike**.
> 1) This happens especially in **rapid speech**, because it makes the words **easier** to say quickly.
> 2) For example, in the word *handbag*, *hand* becomes *ham*, to make it **easier** to **pronounce** with the syllable *bag*.

> **Liaison** is when a **sound** is **inserted between** words or syllables to help them run **together** more smoothly.
> 1) For example — pronouncing /r/ at the **end of words**. When a word ending with **r** is **followed** by a word that **begins** with a **vowel**, the /r/ is **pronounced**, e.g. *mother ate* sounds like *mother rate*.
> 2) This is to avoid a gap between the words, known as **hiatus**.
> 3) Sometimes it's easier to link words with /r/ even if there's no r in the spelling — e.g. *media(r) interest*.

Phonological Frameworks are used to Analyse Sound Patterns

Part of **phonology** involves looking at how sounds can convey **meaning** and **association**.

> 1) **Rhythm** is very clear in **poetry**. Lines are often **constructed** so that the **stress** falls on **important** words, emphasising their meaning, e.g. *But to **go** to **school** in a **summer** morn, / Oh! it **drives** all **joy** away.* **Advertising** also uses rhythm, particularly in **slogans**, to help the audience **remember** the **product**.
>
> 2) **Rhyme** is when words have **similar endings**. It's usually associated with poetry and songs, but it's also used in planned speeches and in advertising. The rhyme words in a speech or text always **stand out**, and their meanings are often **linked**.
>
> 3) **Alliteration** is where two or more words close to each other **begin** with the **same sound**, e.g. *six sizzling sausages*.
>
> 4) **Assonance** is when the **vowel sounds** in the middle of two or more words are similar, e.g. *spoke* and *hope*. When vowel sounds **clash** with each other it's known as **dissonance**.
>
> 5) Alliteration and assonance are used in **creative writing** to **emphasise** words and show that the **meaning** is **linked** in some way. They're also used in **persuasive writing** to make phrases catchy and more memorable.
>
> 6) **Onomatopoeia** — this is when a word **sounds like** the noise it describes, e.g. *buzz, pop, bang, snap*.
>
> 7) Sometimes sounds can appear **symbolic** for other reasons, e.g. **closed vowels** in words like *chip* and *little* can suggest smallness, while **open vowels** in words like *vast* and *grand* can suggest largeness. It's not always the case, but it's worth noting **sound symbolism** like this when you're analysing a text.

Practice Questions

Q1   What is a phoneme? Give examples.
Q2   Give three features of consonants.
Q3   How can pronunciation be affected when words are connected?
Q4   What is the difference between alliteration and assonance?

Essay Question

Q1   How can the techniques of phonetics and phonology be applied in the analysis of a text or speech?

Mobiles, ringtones, texting — this phonology lark is pretty easy...

Apparently when phones were first invented, Alexander Graham Bell thought the best thing to say when you picked up was 'ahoy hoy'. But his rival Thomas Edison didn't like this so he used 'hello' instead, and that's what stuck. I reckon it's about time 'ahoy hoy' made a comeback — remember it next time you answer the phone, and make a poor dead inventor happy.

Cohesion

Cohesion is about connections. Different ideas in a text need to be linked together, otherwise it won't make sense as a whole and you may as well have just smeared some alphabet spaghetti onto the page and claimed it was a short story...

Cohesion refers to the Structure of a Text

1) Cohesion **links ideas** in different parts of a text together.

2) Sometimes texts don't need to be particularly **cohesive** because they rely on **prior knowledge**. In this case the reader is expected to **fill in the gaps**, e.g. *The winter was one of the wettest on record. York was bracing itself.* These sentences don't appear to be connected — they rely on the reader to make a **link** between them. For them to make sense, the reader would have to know that heavy rain often causes flooding, which York is very prone to.

3) Generally, though, if a text isn't cohesive then it won't **make sense**. Cohesion is especially important in texts containing **complex arguments** or **development** of ideas.

4) Spoken language is also **cohesive**. See p.62 for how ideas are linked in prepared and spontaneous speech.

Grammatical Cohesion is about Linking Sentences

There are **five** main types of **grammatical cohesion**.

Reference

1) This involves **third person pronouns** (*he, she, it, they*) and **demonstrative pronouns** (*this, that*).

2) An **anaphoric reference** refers **back** to something that has already been mentioned, e.g.
   - *My grandmother went to university.* ***She*** *wanted to be a teacher.*
     The word *she* is the cohesive link between these sentences, because it refers back to the *grandmother*.
   - *He just couldn't stand ducks.* ***That*** *was the big problem.*
     Here, the cohesive word *that* refers back not to just one word, but the whole previous sentence.

3) References **forward** to something in the **future** are called **cataphoric references**, e.g.
   - *The goat gave* ***the following*** *reasons for its decision.*
     The sentence refers to something that has not actually been said yet, and will follow in the next sentences.

4) Reference to something **outside** the text is called an **exophoric reference**. The demonstrative pronouns refer to something in the **immediate**, **present context** of the utterance e.g. *that* tree over *there* (see p.10).

Identification

1) This is when **determiners** like *the, this* and *that* are used to show that a **noun** has already been mentioned, e.g.
   - *A large lorry blocked the road.* ***The*** *lorry had broken down.*

2) The **indefinite article** *a* is used the first time the lorry is mentioned. After that the **definite article** *the* is used to show that the clause is referring to the same noun.

Ellipsis

1) This is where words are **left out** of a sentence.

2) It's still cohesive if the **earlier** part of the text enables the reader to **supply** the **missing information**, e.g.
   - *His jeans were stained, his jacket was ripped and blood dripped down his face. What a state.*

3) The information given in the first sentence allows the reader to understand the second **incomplete** sentence: *What a state (he was in).*

Conjunctions

1) Conjunctions are words that **connect** different words, phrases and clauses, e.g. *and, because, then, although.*

2) They can be used to **link together** parts of a text and show the **relationship** between them, e.g.
   - *They'd been promised roast chicken* ***and*** *they were looking forward to it,* ***but*** *they were sadly disappointed.*

3) The conjunction *and* connects the second clause with the first clause — it shows that what they were *looking forward to* was *roast chicken*. The conjunction *but* qualifies what was said in the previous clause.

Adverbs

These connect clauses by referencing **space** and **time**, e.g.
   - *We're leaving London* ***tomorrow*** *morning,* ***before*** *the traffic gets bad.*

Cohesion

Lexical Cohesion is about Linking Words

Lexical cohesion links words through **meaning** and **association**, rather than through **grammatical structure**:

Repetition

1) Using the **same word** more than once can link separate sentences, e.g.
   *All we could see was **rain**. Anything would have been better than **rain**.*
2) Ideas can also be linked by using **synonyms** (see p.19) rather than exactly the same word, e.g.
   *He **wandered** slowly towards the building, then **ambled** down the corridor before **loitering** outside the door.*
3) This connects different events in the text, but ensures that there's still **variety**.

Collocation

1) Words that commonly appear together in lexical units are called **collocations**.
2) All **native speakers** of English understand its collocations easily, but non-native speakers might find them a bit bizarre. They are related by **association** rather than through any grammatically based rule.
3) Some words produce predictable collocations — you know what word will follow to complete a phrase because the collocation is so **familiar**, e.g. *neat and tidy*.
4) Collocations like this can't be **rearranged** — you'd always say *neat and tidy* rather than *tidy and neat*.
5) Collocations become well known phrases that are seen as **normal** and **acceptable**, e.g. it's perfectly normal to say *fast asleep*, but not *fast awake*, and *wide awake*, but not *wide asleep*.
6) Some words collocate more **broadly** but can still cause confusion for foreign speakers, e.g. the **verbs** that accompany certain phrases — you *make a mistake* rather than *perform* or *do* one.
7) Collocations aren't usually linked together by **meaning** — only by **familiar association**. You can be *green with envy*, but there's nothing green about envy.
8) Collocations are cohesive because they're **recognisable patterns** to the reader. If a word is paired with one that it doesn't collocate with then the **cohesion** and **fluency** of the statement is lost, e.g. you'd have to **stop and think** about the phrase *diamond clear* if you came across it in a text, because the collocation *crystal clear* is much more familiar.

Layout and Presentation can make a text Cohesive

This is a nice easy one to finish with...

1) **Graphological cohesion** is about making a text **look** cohesive.
2) It's particularly important in writing that's designed to be **persuasive**, e.g. adverts. The aim is to draw the reader's eye to the most important points, and make sure that the text looks **consistent** as a **whole**.
3) This is usually achieved by using the same **typeface** for running text, captions and headings, and by using a cohesive **colour scheme**.

Practice Questions

Q1   List five types of grammatical cohesion.
Q2   Explain how repetition has a cohesive effect on a text.
Q3   Explain what collocation is.

Essay Question

Q1   Find a newspaper and look at the front page. How has cohesion contributed to the meaning of the text?

I'm feeling strangely attracted to this page — must be the links effect...

This cohesion stuff is quite simple really, and these pages are a nice reminder of what to do in your essays too — if they don't have cohesion then they won't make any macaroni sense as a whole cheese. And nobody wants shoes like that he laughed. That might well be the case but there's no need to go on about it now. Good. Glad we've sorted those badgers out.

Pragmatics

It'd be a lot easier if everyone just said what they meant. Although not much fun if it turned out that what everyone meant to say was that they think you smell and they hate your shoes. That's kind of what pragmatics is about.

Pragmatics *is about how language is used in* Social Situations

Pragmatics is the study of the part that language plays in **social situations**.

1) The meaning of what people say **isn't** always as **clear-cut** as it might seem.

2) There are lots of **unwritten social rules** that **prevent** people saying certain things, e.g. you probably wouldn't ask the Queen to '*put the kettle on, love*'.

3) There are also social conventions that make people say things in particular situations, e.g. saying *thank you* when somebody gives you something.

4) Pragmatics looks at **how** people get their **meaning** across within different **social contexts**. People often have to **imply** meanings rather than state them **directly**, so pragmatics concentrates on the meaning **behind** what's actually being said — the **subtext**.

5) It's good to point out when speakers don't address each other as you might **expect** them to, e.g. if family members address each other formally then it might suggest they don't get on and feel uncomfortable around each other.

Prosody *is the* Non-Verbal Aspects *of* Speech

Prosody is about **how** you say things, rather than what you say.
These **non-verbal aspects** of **speech** help **communicate** attitudes and meaning.

'Non-verbal aspects of speech' just means all the aspects of speech that aren't words.

1) **Pitch** — the **level** of the voice is most noticeable if it's particularly **high** or **low**. People might speak with a low pitch if they're relaxed, or depressed. They might speak in a high pitched voice if they're excited or frightened.

2) **Volume** — loudness can show **excitement** or **anger**. **Confident** speakers tend to speak more **loudly** than **nervous** speakers. Speaking quietly can also be a politeness strategy.

3) **Pace** — the **speed** of speaking is another example of non-verbal communication. Slow, controlled speech conveys a sense of calm and authority. Rapid speech can suggest excitement or panic.

4) **Pauses** — pauses can often be **awkward** in conversations, so people often try to fill them. They can show that speakers are **thinking** about what they say, or are **unsure** of themselves.

5) **Intonation** — the same words can mean different things depending on how you say them, so **variation** in tone is important for getting the right meaning across. E.g. you could say something angrily or sarcastically.

6) **Stress** — each word or phrase has a pattern of **stressed** and **unstressed syllables**. This is called **natural stress**. **Changing** the way these words are usually stressed can **change** the **meaning** — **emphatic stress**.

7) **Rhythm** — this is similar to **stress**. Prepared speech often has a more strict rhythmic pattern of **stressed** and **unstressed** syllables than spontaneous speech. This is especially true if the speech has a **persuasive** purpose.

Prosody *can* Change *the* Meaning

1) The way that something is said can completely change its meaning, so looking at **prosodic features** is really important in **pragmatics**.

2) E.g. there are loads of ways of saying this sentence that would **change** its **meaning**:

genuine compliment — *those yellow trousers are nice*

sarcastic

flirtatious   envious   angry

comparative — <u>those</u> yellow trousers are nice (compared to these yellow trousers).

comparative — those <u>yellow</u> trousers are nice (compared to the blue ones).

3) It can be really **difficult** to convey **prosodic features** in **writing**. Writers sometimes use **bolding**, <u>underlining</u> or *italics* to show where the emphasis should be. In fiction, they often have to **explain** how a character says something, e.g. *He answered quickly and angrily.*

Pragmatics

Politeness Strategies ensure speakers Don't Cause Offence

No one knew how to tell Liz that the all-in-one body stocking wasn't a good look.

1) There are lots of **different ways** to communicate an idea. The way you do it depends on the **situation** — where you are and who you're with.

2) You might need to be **tactful** and **diplomatic**, or very **forceful**.

3) People use different **politeness strategies** depending on how they want to come across, even if the **underlying meaning** is still the **same**.

4) Here are some of the possible strategies for saying *no* in response to the question *would you like to go and see a film tonight?*:

Politeness Strategy	Example
Definite with negative word (e.g. *no, not, never*)	*No / no way / not a chance.* This sort of direct response would normally just be used with friends or family, because it's generally thought to be a bit rude.
Definite without negative word	*Are you serious? / I'd rather die.* These could be used for humorous effect, or if you really didn't care about being offensive.
Excuse	*I'd love to but I'm busy / Tonight isn't a very good night.* Excuses are used to justify why the answer is no.
Evasive	*Can we talk about this later / Now's just not a good time.* Evasive responses are used to avoid having to say no.
Apologetic	*Sorry... / I'm afraid...* People often apologise when they're saying no to soften their negative response.
Inarticulate	*Erm / Ah / Hmm* This usually shows that the person feels awkward and is trying to think of an excuse or a way to say no politely. If they stall for long enough, the meaning will become clear anyway.

5) People often use **more than one** politeness strategy in their response, e.g. if they were saying no, they might say *erm sorry no I can't tonight, I'm really busy*.

6) Politeness strategies also act as **conventions** for what to say in certain situations, e.g. it's normal in English to hear shop assistants and customers saying *thank you* to **each other** when a transaction is carried out at a till. Some politeness strategies like this are used **more** in the **UK** than in other countries.

7) Sometimes following the rules of politeness can lead to strategies being used in **strange ways**, e.g. people often say *sorry* when someone else bumps into them in the street.

Practice Questions

Q1 How do social conventions affect the way we speak?

Q2 Describe how prosody can affect meaning.

Q3 Name and describe the six politeness strategies you could use to turn down an invitation.

Essay Question

Q1 Explain how and why people alter the language they use depending on the social situation they're in.

Pragmatics — make sure you Czech your meaning...

This stuff can sound quite obvious, but until you start learning about all these social rules you often don't notice how weird they are. There's no actual law against going up to a stranger, giving them a hug and telling them how much you've missed them, but most people don't do it. It's a shame really — you never know, you might end up making a lovely new friend.

Graphology

Graphology is about what pages look like, and how things like the layout can help get the meaning of the text across. It's a lovely little topic, cos it gives you the chance to talk about pretty doodles and colours and borders.

Layout and Presentation can Emphasise Meaning

1) Text and images can be placed **next to** each other in **effective** ways. This is called **juxtaposition**. For example, **newspapers** might place **similar** stories next to each other on the page. They might also put **adverts** next to stories that they **correspond** with, e.g. an advert for an airline next to an article about holiday destinations.

2) If the **text** is **broken up** with **borders** or **boxes** then it's designed to draw the reader's **attention** to a particular section. It also makes the text seem more **appealing**. **Colour** and **graphics** can have the same effect.

3) It's good to mention whether the layout fits in with the **form**, e.g. you'd expect a newspaper article to have a bold heading and text set out in columns. Sometimes texts adopt the conventions of **different forms** for **effect**, e.g. a newspaper article might be set out like a letter or a diary.

Typeface is often called Font

This is a bit of a confusing one — until everyone started using computers, **typeface** and **font** were seen as completely **different** things.

1) **Typeface** was things like Arial and Times New Roman, and **font** just referred to the size of the text and whether it was **bold** or *italic*.

2) But now the terms tend to be used **interchangeably**, and most people would call these **different fonts** *not* different typefaces.

3) When you're talking about the style of the lettering in the exam, it's probably best to stick to saying **typeface**.

Magda had never seen such a gorgeous typeface.

There are some general things to look out for:

Ascenders and Descenders
- These are the '**stems**' of letters.
- The bits that extend **upwards** are the **ascenders**, on letters like 'd', 'h' and 'l'.
- The bits that extend **downwards** are **descenders**, on letters like 'j', 'q' and 'y'.
- **Long** ascenders and descenders could be used to indicate **sophistication** or **elegance**.

Leading
- This is the amount of **vertical space** between **lines** of type.
- It can affect whether the text is dense and difficult to read, or very spaced out.

Serif
- These are small **strokes** on the **ends** of letters.
- Typefaces that don't include them are called *sans serif* (**without serifs**).
- Typefaces with serifs tend to seem **traditional**, while *sans serif* typefaces are considered more **modern**.

Typeface is used to create Different Effects

In any text the **typeface** has been chosen for a particular **reason**, so you need to consider the **effect** it has.

1) The choice of **typeface** tells you about the **tone** of the text. Typefaces can seem traditional, informal, youthful, elegant, etc. They can be can be made to look like handwriting, for example.

2) Bold, italics and underlining can place **emphasis** on certain parts of the text to show that it's **important**.

3) The use of **upper** and **lower case** letters can also be significant. Words can be **capitalised** to draw attention to them. Sometimes the typeface is all **lower case**, which can appear **stylish**, **modern** or **experimental**.

Graphology

Graphemes are Units in a Writing System

1) **Graphemes** are the **smallest units** that can create **contrasts** in **meaning**, e.g. letters of the alphabet like <f> and <e>, and symbols like <,> and <&>.

2) For linguistic analysis they're usually written in **angle brackets** — e.g. <m>, <?>.

3) They can appear in loads of **different** forms, depending on things like **typeface** and **handwriting style**, e.g. <a> can be written as A *A* **a** *a* etc.

4) A different form of a grapheme is called a **glyph**. When **different glyphs** can be used for the **same grapheme**, e.g. A *A* **a** *a* for the grapheme <a>, then they're called **allographs**.

5) Most **graphemes** don't mean anything on their own — their role is to **combine** and **contrast**.

6) However, some **graphemes** can be **interpreted** in **more than one way**, so the **context** they're used in is important:

For example, <x> has many uses — it can mean:

> **EXAMPLE:**
> - A **kiss** at the end of a letter.
> - An **incorrect answer**.
> - For **adults only** — X-rated.
> - '**Illiterate**' when it's used on a form in place of someone's name.
> - '**Location**' — X marks the spot.
> - An indication of **choice**, e.g. when a **ballot paper** is marked with an x.

Graphics can Convey Meaning

1) Graphics can be cartoons, illustrations, tables, photographs and diagrams.

2) Graphics can **break up** the layout of **dense text**, making it more accessible and less formal.

3) They're usually **visual representations** of the text, which help to **illustrate** and **develop** its meaning.

4) They might have the simple **function** of making the meaning **clearer**. This is especially true of **instructional texts** which often use diagrams, and **children's texts**, which might be illustrated to help children learn to read.

5) They could also be used to set the **tone** of a piece, e.g. a cartoon might be used to add humour.

6) Sometimes a graphic will be a deliberate **contrast** to the text, e.g. in a parody or satirical piece of writing.

Don't dwell on graphics for too long — make sure you talk about language by linking your analysis to the text.

Practice Questions

Q1 Give four effects that using different typefaces can create.

Q2 What is a grapheme?

Q3 What function can graphics have in a text?

Essay Question

Q1 Look at two different newspapers, one tabloid and one broadsheet. Analyse the effect of graphological features like typeface and graphics, and the relationship they have with the text.

This is a nightmare — I can barely remember how to draw a bar chart...

It's one of those cruel ironies — you can harp on all you like about how colours and borders can help emphasise meaning, and how a picture paints a thousand words, but the minute you choose to answer your exam in cartoon form, or perhaps create a little flip book in the corners to help get your point across, suddenly everyone changes their tune...

Register

I always wondered why my teachers never replied to my letters. Then I read these pages and found out that the type of language you use should vary depending on what's appropriate to the situation. It's been pretty awkward ever since...

Register is the Type of Language used in different Situations

Registers are the different **varieties** of language used in different **situations**. Deciding which register is **appropriate** to use depends on several factors.

Audience
- This is to do with the **relationship** between the speaker or writer and the audience.
- E.g. if the speaker or writer knows the audience personally, the **register** they use will usually be quite **informal**. It might include informal lexis, like slang and abbreviations (see p.16-17 for more on lexis).
- This may be more apparent in informal speech than in informal writing.

Purpose
- E.g. a **report** will use a **formal register**, as its **purpose** is to convey information accurately.
- When the purpose is more **persuasive**, e.g. an advert, the register will often be more **informal** as the text needs to get the audience's attention in order to persuade them.

Field
- This is the subject being talked about.
- E.g. if the topic is **football**, the **lexis** will include words linked to football, like *match, penalty*, etc.
- Some fields have a larger specialist lexicon (stock of words), like **biochemistry**. Most workplaces have their own lexicon connected solely with that field, from car repair shops to hospitals (see p.40-41 for more on occupational language).

Form
- E.g. business letters will be written in a **formal register** because of the **professional context**. Text messages, on the other hand, tend to use a more **informal register**, as the context is generally social.

Whether the register is **appropriate** depends on the **context** it's used in — using an **informal register** in a **formal situation** is **inappropriate** because it could seem **disrespectful** or **rude**. Using **formal language** in an **informal situation** could sound **unfriendly** and **stuffy**.

Registers Vary in terms of Lexis, Grammar and Phonology

Different **registers** use different **lexis** and **grammar**, and the way they're **pronounced** can **vary** too. For example:

Lexis
- A conversation between two **specialists** would contain **technical vocabulary** that they would both understand. (see p.40-41 for more on occupational language).
- For example, the lexis in the registers used by **mechanical** and **medical** specialists would be very different.

Grammar
- **Register** can affect syntax — the **structure** of clauses and **complexity** of sentences.
- Some registers even have grammatical constructions that are **specific** to them, like the legal register (known as **legalese**), which has lots of clauses and mainly passive sentences.

Phonology
- This is to do with how the words in a particular **register** are **pronounced**.
- The **informal register** people use when speaking to friends involves things like dropping the <h> from words like *have* and missing a <g> off words like *thinking*.
- Generally speaking, the more **formal** a situation is the more likely people are to **modify** their **accent** so it's closer to **Received Pronunciation** (see p.35).

Modes

Modes can be Written or Spoken

There are two main types of mode — written and spoken.

Written modes

1) Written modes include letters, essays, novels, recipes and reports. Written modes tend to be the **most formal**.

2) In written modes the words have to make the **meaning** clear, because there's no opportunity for **non-verbal communication** between the writer and the reader.

3) Sometimes writers try to convey **prosodic features** like tone, intonation and pitch to make the meaning clearer, using **features** like *italicising*, underlining, CAPITALISATION, and **punctuation** like exclamation marks.

Spoken modes

1) Spoken modes are things like interviews, broadcasts and presentations. Spontaneous speech (like conversations between friends) is normally the **least formal** mode.

2) In **spoken modes** speakers can rely on **non-verbal communication** like gestures and **prosodic features** (see p.26) to get their point across.

3) The grammar of informal speech is often **disjointed** — it contains lots of **self-correction**, **interruption** and **incomplete sentences**. It also contains **non-fluency features** (things that interrupt the flow of speech) like **pauses**, **repetition**, **fillers** (*you know, sort of, I mean*) and **false starts**.

4) Speech also tends to contain **phatic expressions** (small talk expressions that have a **social function**, so their meaning isn't particularly important, like *hello* and *how's things*.

Multi-Modal Texts contain Features of both Speech and Writing

Lots of texts are a **mixture** of **spoken** and **written** modes, especially electronic texts like **emails** and **text messages**.

1) These are all **written modes** that can contain elements of **spoken language**, e.g. **phatic communication** like *hello* and *bye*.

2) Very **informal** emails or messages between friends contain **phonetic spellings**, like *b4* for *before*, and *u* for *you*.

3) **Formal** business emails still tend to be **less formal** than **letters** — they tend not to use **conventions** like writing the sender's address at the top. **Paragraphs** and **sentences** tend to be much **shorter**.

Practice Questions

Q1 Outline three factors that influence which register is used.

Q2 How can registers vary in terms of phonology?

Q3 Name three differences between spoken and written modes.

Essay Question

Q1 Discuss how and why writers employ different registers in different situations, giving examples.

't shouldn't be the mode difficult thing to underdand...

Modes, continuums, typology... I don't know when it all became so complicated. Makes you long for a time when all you had to worry about was sitting on the mat and watching Words and Pictures. Then a bag of crisps for morning break, a bit of a play in the sand, and home before 3.30. Yes, life really was much better back in year 11...

Accent and Dialect

English isn't just spoken or written in one way — imagine how boring that would be. Instead, there are loads of different varieties. These pages are all about dialect and accent — basically, what you say and how you say it...

Accents *are* Variations *in* Pronunciation

1) **English** words can be **pronounced** in different ways. The different **patterns** of pronunciation are called **accents**.

2) Accents can be affected by the speaker's **regional** or **social** background.

3) An accent can be a feature of a dialect. But it's **different** to **dialect** because it just refers to **how** you say words, not the words themselves.

You need to consider accents when you look at the phonology of spoken language (see p.22-23).

> 1) Pronunciation and intonation can vary over **large geographic areas** like countries, e.g. the difference between American, Australian and English.
>
> 2) In **England**, most people can tell the difference between **northern accents** and **southern accents**. The main differences are between **vowel sounds**, e.g.
> Someone with a **northern accent** would say *path* with a short vowel sound, to sound like *cat*.
> Someone with a **southern accent** would say *parth*, with a long vowel sound.
>
> 3) Sometimes people that live near each other can tune in to **smaller** differences in each other's accents, to the point where you can often tell if someone's from your town or one a few miles away.

Dialects *are* Variations *in* Language

1) A **dialect** is a **variation** in a language, with its own distinctive features of **vocabulary**, **grammar** and **pronunciation**. It's different to **accent** because it refers to the **specific words** you use, not just **how** you **say** them.

2) The term **dialect** is usually used to describe language that's particular to a specific **geographical region**.

3) It's also sometimes used as a **general** term for variations in language that are the result of **social background** (**sociolect** — see p.36) or **personal differences** (**idiolect** — see p.37).

> ### Vocabulary
> Different dialects have different words for things, e.g.
>
> > - Someone from Yorkshire might say *anyroad* for *anyway*.
> > - People in Lancashire might call a *bread roll* a *barm*.
> > - In the West Country *acker* means *friend*.
> > - In East Anglia to *mardle* is to *gossip*.

> ### Grammar
> The way that people form sentences can depend on their dialect. Regional dialects often contain **non-standard** grammar (see p.34), e.g.
>
> > - *them* as a demonstrative adjective — *look at **them** books*
> > - Double negatives — *we **don't** want **none***
> > - Missing plurals — *it costs four **pound***
> > - Missing the *-ly* suffix off the end of adverbs — *I walked **slow***
>
> Some grammatical variations are **specific** to a **particular** dialect, e.g. people from **Yorkshire** might miss out the definite article *the*, so they might say *I cleaned car* rather than *I cleaned **the** car*. The **Scouse** dialect has *youse* as the plural of *you* — e.g. *what are youse doing?*

> ### Pronunciation
> 1) Most regional dialects have an **accent** to go with them. So you'd probably expect a **Geordie** (someone from Newcastle) to say the word *town* like *toon*, or someone from **Cornwall** to pronounce the *r* in *water*.
>
> 2) But don't forget — accents are just **one feature** of a dialect. You can use words and constructions from one dialect but speak in the accent of another.

Accent and Dialect

People Have Different Attitudes towards Accents and Dialects

People sometimes make assumptions about others based on the variety of English they use, e.g. people from the **north** of England often think that people with **southern accents** sound 'posh'.

1) **Workman (2008)** studied people's **perceptions** of different **accents**. Participants listened to recordings of different accents while they looked at photos of people.

2) It was found that participants rated the **intelligence** of the people in the photos differently, depending on which accent they thought they had.

3) **Yorkshire** accents were rated as sounding the **most intelligent**. When a recording of a **Birmingham** accent was played, the people in the photo were rated as being much **less intelligent**. Obviously this **isn't** actually **true**, but it shows how strong the **stereotypes** about different accents can be.

Someone's **accent** or **dialect** is often a good indication of **where they're from**. But it can also provide clues about their **social background** and **education**.

1) **Standard English** (p.34) is a **social dialect**. It's usually associated with **educated**, **middle** and **upper class** people. It's the way that you're taught to use English at school, and the language of **formal speech** and **writing**.

2) Some people **assume** that people who use **regional dialects** are **less well educated**, or **lower class**.

3) On the other hand, **regional varieties** of English are often associated with being **down-to-earth** and **modest**, e.g. there are now lots of TV presenters with regional accents, because their accents are seen as being more **accessible** to audiences (see p.35).

You need to look at Written Language as well

Dialect and accent don't just apply to **spoken language**.

1) **Transcripts** of speech can show features of **regional dialects**. Look out for dialect words and grammatical constructions, e.g. *we **seen** her yesterday with her **bairns***.

2) **Literary texts** can contain representations of **accents** as well as **dialects**. The author has included these features for a reason — the way characters speak **reflects** something about them. For example, in *Oliver Twist* by **Charles Dickens**, the Artful Dodger says to Oliver "*I've got to be in London to-night; and I know a '**spectable** old **genelman** as lives there, **wot'll** give you lodgings for **nothink***". These features imply things about the character, e.g. that he's from London and he's lower class.

3) Some literary texts are written **entirely** in a **regional dialect**, rather than **Standard English**. This is called **dialect literature**. Authors do this for different reasons, e.g. to make the story seem more **authentic** and **realistic**, or to make a statement about attitudes towards regional varieties of English.

Practice Questions

Q1 What is the difference between accent and dialect?
Q2 Give two examples of how regional dialects can vary from Standard English.
Q3 Outline some of the different attitudes that people sometimes have towards regional accents and dialects.

Essay Question

"I mean as 'appen Ah can find anuther pleece as'll du for rearin' th' pheasants. If yo' want ter be 'ere, yo'll non want me messin' abaht a' t' time."
She looked at him, getting his meaning through the fog of the dialect.
"Why don't you speak ordinary English?" she said coldly.
"Me! — Ah thowt it *wor*' ordinary."

From *Lady Chatterley's Lover*, by DH Lawrence

Q1 Identify some features of regional dialect, and explain what the author is suggesting about attitudes towards them.

Ain't naw use twinin bout revision — quit yer mitherin and gerronwi'it...

It's best to think of English like a family-sized variety pack of crisps, full of different flavours. Scouse and Onion, Salt and Lancashire, Prawn Cockneytail (that's a good one) — they're all here for you to crunch loudly in your dad's ear while he's trying to watch the news. Yes, with its tasty potato-based dialects and crinkle-cut accents, English really is the king of snacks...

Standard English and RP

By now you've probably realised that there are loads of different varieties of English. So many, in fact, that it's a wonder people can understand each other. But they can, and it's down to a little thing called standardisation...

Standard English is a Social Dialect

Standard English is a dialect of English. It has distinctive features of **vocabulary**, **grammar** and **spelling**.

1) A **standard** form of a language is one that is considered to be **acceptable** or correct by **educated** speakers.

2) In **medieval England** people in different parts of the country spoke very different **dialects**. They were so varied that people from different regions would have had **difficulty understanding** each other.

3) The **Standard English** used today started off as the **regional dialect** of the East Midlands. Its influence spread around the country, and it became the dialect that was used in print.

4) As more books were printed, **variations** in **spelling** and **grammar** were ironed out — the language started to conform towards a **standard**.

5) People began to **codify** the language (decide how to write it) in **dictionaries** and books of **grammar rules**. For example, Johnson's dictionary, printed in 1755, aimed to standardise spellings and word meanings.

6) The standard form of the language became associated with **education**, **class** and **power**.

> It's difficult to give examples of **Standard English** as a dialect, because it's what other dialects are usually compared with. As a general example though, this book is written in Standard English, as it contains mostly **standardised vocabulary**, **spellings** and **syntax**.

Standard English is used in Lots of Situations

Standard English is the most widely understood version of English, so it's used in lots of different fields:

1) **Education** — Standard English is the variety of English taught in schools, and it's what people are taught when they learn English as a foreign language.

2) **Media** — it's used in newspapers and by newsreaders on the TV.

3) **Formal documents** — it's the language used in essays, business letters and reports.

4) **Formal speech** — you'd expect people to speak using Standard English in formal situations like business negotiations and public announcements.

People have Different Attitudes towards Standard English

1) As one variety of the language became standardised, other varieties became seen as **less prestigious**.

2) **Regional dialects** were associated with the **uneducated** and the **lower classes**, so it was seen as important to be able to use English '**properly**' if you wanted to be successful.

> **Standard English** is often seen as the '**correct**' or '**pure**' form of the language. Other varieties are sometimes thought to be '**corruptions**' of it. There's a view that if you use another dialect, you're not using English '**properly**'.

> However, most **linguists** argue that all varieties of English should be **valued equally**. There's **no reason** why Standard English should be seen as better than any other dialect. They claim that people shouldn't be thought of as **uneducated** or **lower class** if they **don't** use Standard English.

Standard English and RP

Received Pronunciation (RP) is a Social Accent

1) **Received Pronunciation** is an **accent**, traditionally associated with **educated** people and the **upper classes**.

2) This means it's **different** to other accents, which normally indicate which **region** the speaker's from.

3) Traditionally **RP** and **Standard English** are linked — the most **prestigious** way of speaking would be Standard English using RP. While lots of people speak Standard English (or something close) with regional accents, you don't generally hear people saying dialect words and phrases in RP.

Emma had just received some very juicy pronunciation.

4) The most recognisable examples of RP are how the **Queen** speaks, and the traditional speech of **BBC presenters**. Because of this, people sometimes refer to RP as the **Queen's English**, or **BBC English**.

5) Because RP has been seen as the standard, accepted way of speaking English, it's the accent many people are taught to use when they learn English as a **foreign language**.

> **Some features of RP**
> - **Long vowel** sounds in words like *grass* (grarss) and *castle* (carstle).
> - **Long vowel** sound in words like *come* and *under*.
> - Pronouncing **h**s and **t**s in words like *hat* and *letter*.

RP has Changed Over Time

Language is always changing, and nowadays very few people actually use RP in its 'original' form, e.g. BBC newsreaders use **Standard English**, but they speak it in a range of **regional accents**. Even the Queen's accent has changed a bit from when she was first crowned 50 years ago.

> **Estuary English**
>
> 1) Some linguists claim that **RP** is being replaced as the most 'acceptable' English accent by **Estuary English**. This is an **accent** that has roots in the speech found around the **Thames Estuary** in **London**.
>
> 2) It contains many similar features to the **Cockney** accent, e.g. dropping **h**s at the beginning of words (pronouncing *hit* like *it*), and pronouncing **th** like **f** (so *mouth* becomes *mouff*).
>
> 3) It's used by a lot of people in the **entertainment industry**, as it's seen as a **commercially acceptable** accent.
>
> 4) Because of the **influence** of the **media**, Estuary English is becoming increasingly common **outside** of London. You can't necessarily tell where someone's from if they use Estuary English — it's become a **widespread accent**.

Practice Questions

Q1   Identify which of the following statements are in Standard English and which aren't.   Explain why.
'I were going home when I spotted 'im.'
'The circumference of the circle ain't 54.'
'Turn left at the end of the road. Then take a sharp right.'

Q2   What factors contributed to the rise of Standard English as the accepted dialect?

Q3   Name four instances when you might use Standard English.

Q4   What is RP?

Essay Question

Q1   The use of Standard English and RP in the media has changed over the last 50 years. Identify some of these changes and comment on why they might have taken place.

wivowt stndrd inglish we cudnt undrstnd eech uvver...

Aha, I've done something rather clever there — I've shown that we can still understand each other even without Standard English. That's OK, there's no need to applaud, it's all in a day's work. It does make you wonder why people bang on about using 'good English' so much though, and whether it's right that one variety should be seen as better than the others...

Sociolect and Idiolect

Every individual uses language in a slightly different way. You don't spend all your time talking to yourself in the bathroom mirror, so it makes sense that the way you speak is affected by who you're with and what you're doing.

Sociolect is the Language of Social Groups

Sociolects (or **social dialects**) are **varieties** of language used by particular **social groups**, e.g. middle-aged lawyers speak differently from school children. The sociolects of different groups help to give them their own **identities**.

The language people use depends on different social factors:

> *The points in this section are generalisations, so they're not true for everyone.*

Socio-economic status
* Studies have shown that **middle** and **upper class** people tend to use more **standard forms** (see p.34-35) than **lower class** people.
* The language of lower class people is more likely to contain features of **regional dialect** (p.32-33).

Education
* Studies show that **well-educated** people are more likely to use **Standard English** and **RP** (see p.34-35) than less well-educated people.
* They're usually less likely to use words and sentence structures from **regional dialects**.

Age
* Sociolects used by teenagers tend to include more **non-standard** forms and **slang** (p.38-39) than language used by adults.
* They also include more influences from, and references to, **popular culture**.

Occupation (there's more on language and occupation on p.40-41)
* Every occupation has its own specialist terms and technical vocabulary, known as **jargon**.
* You might expect a lawyer to talk about *tort* (a civil wrong) or *GBH* (grievous bodily harm), and a doctor to talk about *prescriptions* or *scrubs*.
* Sometimes these **sociolects** also have distinctive **grammatical** features, e.g. legal documents often contain **complex** sentences with lots of subordinate clauses.

Belief system and culture
* **Religious groups** use lots of **specialist vocabulary**, e.g. *Diwali* (the Hindu festival of light), *kosher* (food prepared in accordance with Jewish law), *salah* (Islamic daily prayers).
* Because UK society is **multicultural**, lots of words from other languages and cultures have become part of a **wider** sociolect.
* For example, the word *kosher* isn't just used by members of the Jewish community. It's taken on a **broader** meaning in the English language, so people often use it to mean *allowed* or *acceptable*.

The Way you Speak can Depend on the Situation

Language that's **appropriate** in one social group might not be appropriate in another. People **adapt** the way they speak depending on the **situation** they're in, and how they want to present themselves. For example:

1) **Politicians** tend to use **Standard English** when they're making a political speech, because they're in a formal situation. But when they're talking to individuals on the street they might use **non-standard** language and features of **regional dialect**, so that they seem down-to-earth.

2) Lots of people find that the way they speak to their **friends** is different from how they speak to their **parents**. They might use more **slang** with their friends, or speak in the same **regional dialect** as their parents when they're at home.

3) Some people have a **telephone voice** — a different voice that they use on the phone. Usually it involves using more **standard** forms and an accent that's closer to **Received Pronunciation**.

"Hello? Yes, I'd like to speak to a Mr Hugh Jass".

Sociolect and Idiolect

Idiolect is the Unique Language of an Individual

1) The word choices that people make, and the way they form sentences, are specific to them.

2) This means that the way you use language can **identify** you, like a **fingerprint**.

3) Your **idiolect** is the result of a **unique combination** of **influences**.

Where you're from

- Where you're from affects how you speak. You might expect a person from Newcastle to have a Geordie **accent** and use **dialect** words like *gan* for *go*.

- But not everyone from the same **area** speaks in exactly the **same** way.

- A person could have **moved** from somewhere else and so **retained** aspects of **other** regional accents and dialects.

Social background

- The way you speak is also influenced by your **social background** (**sociolect** — see the previous page).

- Your sociolect is the **product** of lots of different **factors** such as socio-economic status, age, religious beliefs, education, and gender.

- It's also affected by influences from **smaller** social groups, e.g. schools, sports teams and groups of friends.

"By 'eck, lad, this is a crackin' spread. Now pass us another growler."

Personal characteristics

- The language a person uses could be affected by aspects of their **personality**.

- For example, a **nervous** person might use sentences with lots of **fillers** (*um, like, sort of* etc.).

Practice Questions

Q1 What is a sociolect?

Q2 Give four examples of social groups that might have their own sociolect.

Q3 How might the situation you're in affect the way you speak?

Q4 What is an idiolect?

Q5 Give three factors that might influence a person's idiolect.

Essay Question

Q1 What can a person's use of language reveal about their identity?

You could comment on group influence, accent, dialect, slang, and social background.

Idiolect — the opposite of intellect...

You might have realised by now that speech is a bit of a witch's brew — a foul concoction made up of dialect, sociolect and a pinch of accent, all stirred together and simmered gently under the light of the full moon. After twenty minutes take it off the heat, rinse around the gums, gargle, spit, and hey presto! A fun new voice to amaze your friends and family...

Slang

Yeah yeah, don't think I don't know what you're up to — these pages are not to be used by people who just want to have a giggle at some naughty words. (I'd suggest that you use the dictionary for that — it's a lot more fun...)

Slang is Informal Vocabulary

1) **Slang** refers to **informal**, **non-standard** words and expressions that tend to be used in **casual speech**.

2) It's often **inventive** and **creative**, and enters the language in lots of different ways.

New meanings for existing words	**Shortening existing words**	**New words**
• *cool, wicked* — good	• *telly* — television	• *moolah* — money
• *sad* — pathetic	• *rents* — parents	• *yonks* — a long time, ages
• *chick* — girl	• *mare* — nightmare	• *snog* — kiss

Slang has Different Purposes

1) People tend to use slang to **identify** that they're part of a particular **social group** — it's part of their **sociolect** (see p.36). Using particular slang shows that you **fit in** and suggests **shared values**.

2) Slang can act as a code to **exclude outsiders**, e.g. groups of teenagers might use slang to establish a sense of identity which is separate from the adult world. It can be **exclusive** and **secretive**.

3) Some of the main **purposes** of using **slang** are to be **rebellious** or **entertaining**.

> **Slang and social taboos**
>
> • Subjects that there's lots of **slang** for are often **social taboos** — things that are thought of as **inappropriate** or **unacceptable** to talk about in formal social situations, e.g. words for sex, sex organs and bodily functions.
>
> • Some of the most common and most offensive slang words are **swear words**.
>
> • It's seen as **taboo** to swear in some situations, e.g. in class at school. In this case the purpose of swearing is to be **rebellious**.
>
> • In other situations swearing is an **accepted** part of a group's **sociolect**, and people do it to **fit in** and be **entertaining**, e.g. when they're talking with a group of friends.
>
> • Not all **slang** is **taboo language**, but there's a lot **more** slang for **taboo subjects** than for any others.

Slang is Specific to Social and Regional Groups

1) Some slang words are **familiar** to **lots of speakers**, e.g. most people in the UK probably know that **tenner** is short for **ten pounds**.

2) However, slang also **varies** depending on which **region** speakers are from. Sometimes it's difficult to distinguish slang words from regional dialect variants.

3) One example of **regional slang** is **Cockney rhyming slang**, e.g. *butcher's hook* — **look**.

4) The slang a person uses also depends on **social factors**, e.g. a middle class speaker will probably speak something close to **Standard English** and use fewer slang words than a working class speaker.

5) Some slang is only used by very **small social groups**, like a particular school or group of friends.

6) Slang reflects **multiculturalism**, as slang terms can come from lots of different cultures, e.g. **tucker** — an Australian slang word for food.

7) The **media** also influences slang and gives people **access** to different subcultures.

> • British **youth** culture has been particularly influenced by **African American** slang, through popular music and TV.
>
> • **Hip hop culture** has introduced black American slang that lots of English speakers now recognise, e.g. *sick* — good, *bling* — flashy jewellery, *crib* — house.

Slang

Slang *is always* Changing

Slang changes very quickly as words go in and out of **fashion**.

1) There are lots of slang words that used to be popular, that you don't hear any more, e.g. *cove* — man, *beak* — magistrate, *viz* — face, *cits* — citizens.

2) Slang terms can quickly start to sound **dated**, e.g. *mega* — good, *dweeb* — someone who isn't cool. This happens especially with **teenage slang** that becomes more **mainstream** when adults and young children start using it, which causes teenagers to stop using it.

3) Sometimes slang terms become so widely used that they become part of **Standard English**, e.g. *okay*, *phone* and *bus*. These words were once considered **informal**, but now it would seem formal to say *telephone*, and very unusual to say *omnibus*.

4) The **opposite** can also happen — words can go from being formal or acceptable, to being classed as vulgar. An example of this is the word *arse*, which wasn't thought of as informal until the 17th century.

People have **Different Attitudes** towards **Slang**

Slang is sometimes seen as **low level**, **vulgar** language, which shouldn't be used in **writing** or in **formal situations**.

1) Some people think that if you use slang you're **undermining standards** by not using the language '**properly**'. They assume that people who use lots of slang are lower class and uneducated.

2) Slang is seen as the language of **informal speech**, so it's considered **inappropriate** to use it in a **formal context**, e.g. you'd lose marks if you wrote an essay using slang words and phrases.

3) This is because slang has a reputation for being **rebellious** and **subversive**, so it isn't formally accepted as a variety of English. Some people worry it doesn't follow the 'proper' **spelling** and **grammar rules** of **Standard English**.

4) However, most slang words and phrases **do** follow the rules of Standard English — they're just more flexible.

5) People who are interested in slang argue that it's an **intelligent** and **creative** variety of language, which **changes** and **develops** very quickly. It also serves an important **social purpose** — people use it to **identify** themselves as part of a **group**.

Practice Questions

Q1 Identify which word in each pair is slang, and which is Standard English:

Old Bill / police, upset / gutted, tired / knackered, quids in / wealthy, lucky / jammy

Q2 Give two reasons why people might use slang.

Q3 Explain two ways in which slang can change over time.

Essay Question

A: yeah I had a well good time (.) just really chilled (2.0) just sat on my arse all day

B: wish I had (.) Gemma was being a bitch again (.) I had to keep nipping off to phone her

A: it's not on

B: tell me about it (1.0) I wanna be like your attitude stinks but she'll just blank me till I cave in so what you gonna do

A: chuck her (.) she ain't worth it

It's normal for transcripts not to have any punctuation. Instead, (.) indicates a short pause. Numbers in brackets indicate the length of a pause in seconds.

Q1 Identify the different types of slang used in this extract and comment on the purpose it serves.

Cripes chums — learning about slang is smashingly wizard...

Good old Eng Lang — there aren't many subjects where you get the chance to discuss the ins and outs (oo-er) of swearing like this. Although I suppose the point of rude words is that they're not quite as fun if you're allowed to use them. Few things are likely to raise more of a snigger than slipping words like knockers into an exam answer...

Language and Occupational Groups

Ever wondered why you never hear plumbers talking about PSHE or teachers talking about siphon-vortex water closets? No, me neither, but it's something to do with occupational sociolects — the specific language of occupational groups...

Different Occupations have their Own Sociolects

1) **Occupational sociolect** is the distinctive language used by particular occupational groups, e.g. lawyers or train drivers (see p.36).

2) It's found in **spoken** and **written** forms.

3) The **sociolect** develops to fit the group's **specific purposes** — it's not **everyday** language.

4) **Specialists** in a job use it to communicate **quickly** and **precisely** with other specialists in the **same job**. You wouldn't necessarily expect **non-specialists** to understand it.

5) Occupational language can be seen as **elitist** — **excluding** people who **don't understand** it.

Occupational Language has a Special Lexis

Occupational words are the **specialist terms** used in specific jobs — often called **jargon** (see p.52). They can refer to **concepts**, **processes**, **conditions**, **roles** or **objects**. For example:

- **Hairstylists** might say — *perm, feather, spritz, weave, layer, trim*.
- **Electricians** might say — *transformer, faceplate, fuse, amp, earth*.
- **Actors** might say — *role, script, agent, motivation, scene*.

These words might **not** be **familiar** to people **outside** the occupational group.

Police officers might say —
"you put your left leg in, your
left leg out..."

Occupational Language has Distinctive Grammatical Features

1) When you're analysing the grammatical features of occupational language, focus on elements like **word classes**, **syntax**, and **sentence functions**.

2) The example below is from a **medical report** written by specialists, to be read by other specialists:

> *A 27-year-old female **presented with** a pneumothorax, which progressed into **rapidly degenerative Bronchiolitis Obliterans Organising Pneumonia**.*

These aren't general features of all occupational language — the grammar used in different occupations varies.

- **Word classes** — the **past participle** *presented* is used in an unusual way. It's combined with the preposition **with** to create a **prepositional verb** which describes the **symptoms** the patient was showing.

  The **head word** *pneumonia* has **premodifiers** in front of it — the **adverb** *rapidly* and the **adjective** *degenerative*. This makes the sentence grammatically complex.

- **Syntax** — the long **noun phrase** '*Bronchiolitis Obliterans Organising Pneumonia*' is common in this type of medical writing. It packs as much complex information as possible into a small space.

- **Function** — the text's **function** is to **give information**, so it only contains **declarative sentences** (see p.15).

Occupational Language can have Distinctive Phonological Features

Some kinds of occupational language have **phonological** features like **repetition**, **alliteration** and **rhyme** (see p.23).

1) You usually find distinctive **phonological features** in the language of occupations where it's necessary to speak to **large groups** of people, e.g. **politician**, **religious leader**, **teacher**.

2) This example from a **political speech** uses **alliteration** and **phonological patterning** with a **three part list**, e.g. *we will bring you **peace**, **pride** and **prosperity** like you've never experienced before*.

3) Teachers' language might have some common **prosodic features** when they're addressing classes, e.g. they're more likely to raise their voices or say *shh*.

Language and Occupational Groups

Occupational Language Varies depending on its Form and Function

1) **Written** occupational discourse has lots of different **forms**, e.g. legal contracts and business letters.

2) **Spoken** occupational discourse also takes different **forms**, e.g. a counsellor might use gentle questioning, a sergeant major might shout out imperatives, and a politician might use rhetorical questions.

3) Occupational discourse also has a variety of **functions** depending on its **context**. For example:

> - **informative discourse**, e.g. a manager explaining a task to an employee.
> - **persuasive discourse**, e.g. a charity worker asking for donations.
> - **instructional discourse**, e.g. an experienced plumber advising an apprentice.
> - **transactional discourse**, e.g. a retailer buying from a wholesaler.

4) Some discourse has a **mixture** of functions, e.g. a factory's health and safety manual might be designed to **inform**, **instruct** and **persuade**.

Occupational Discourse can follow a Specific Structure

This sounds more complicated than it is — basically, it's just looking at the **order** the discourse takes, and how it can be separated by **discourse markers**. For example:

1) **Scientific reports** have a specific structure — **title, introduction, method, findings, conclusion, evaluation**. These **standard headings** act as **discourse markers** by organising it in a specific order.

2) A police officer arresting somebody follows a strict **verbal discourse structure**: *you do not have to say anything, but it may harm your defence if you do not mention when questioned something that you later rely on in court.*

> In this example of a teacher's report on a pupil, the discourse is structured in **four parts**:
>
> > *Ferdinand is doing well in Mathematics and has made significant progress. However, he really must apply himself next term if he is to fulfil his potential.*
>
> 1. Present performance — *is doing well* (**present continuous tense**).
> 2. Past to present performance — *has made significant progress* (**present perfect tense**).
> 3. What he has to do — *he really must apply himself* (**use of modal**).
> 4. Success depends on him doing this — *if he is to fulfil his potential* (**conditional clause**).
>
> Here the **adverb** *however* acts as a **discourse marker**. It gives the text an **order** by **linking** what's happened in the **past** with what needs to happen in the **future**.

Practice Questions

Q1 What is meant by the term occupational sociolect?
Q2 Give three examples of 'occupation-specific' lexis.
Q3 Give three types of grammatical features you should analyse in occupational language.
Q4 Name three kinds of phonological features that can sometimes be found in occupational language.
Q5 Give an example of one form and one function of occupational discourse.

Essay Question

Q1 Outline the main features of occupational language, and the specific purposes it serves.

You could focus on lexis, grammar, phonological features, form, function and structure.

At least all this revision will keep you occupied...

This is another topic where it can feel like you're stating the obvious quite a lot — you wouldn't really expect, say, doctors to spend much time talking about leather uppers and shoelaces. Well, not while they were at work. Unless someone had had a bizarre accident with a pair of brogues... But that's beside the point. This is all nice simple stuff, so fear not.

Sources and Exam Questions

This is an exam-style question, based on sources like the ones you'll get in the real paper.

Texts A–E illustrate different varieties of language use.

Discuss various ways in which these texts can be grouped, giving reasons for your choices. [48]

Text A — from *Lady Windermere's Fan,* by Oscar Wilde

DUMBY	Clever woman, Mrs. Erlynne.
CECIL GRAHAM	Hallo, Dumby! I thought you were asleep.
DUMBY	I am, I usually am!
LORD AUGUSTUS	A very clever woman. Knows perfectly well what a demmed fool I am — knows it as well as I do myself.

[CECIL GRAHAM *comes towards him laughing*.]

	Ah, you may laugh, my boy, but it is a great thing to come across a woman who thoroughly understands one.
DUMBY	It is an awfully dangerous thing. They always end by marrying one.
CECIL GRAHAM	But I thought, Tuppy, you were never going to see her again! Yes! you told me so yesterday evening at the club. You said you'd heard —

[*Whispering to him*.]

LORD AUGUSTUS	Oh, she's explained that.
CECIL GRAHAM	And the Wiesbaden affair?
LORD AUGUSTUS	She's explained that too.
DUMBY	And her income, Tuppy? Has she explained that?
LORD AUGUSTUS	[*In a very serious voice.*] She's going to explain that to-morrow.

[CECIL GRAHAM *goes back to C. table*.]

DUMBY	Awfully commercial, women nowadays. Our grandmothers threw their caps over the mills, of course, but, by Jove, their granddaughters only throw their caps over mills that can raise the wind for them.
LORD AUGUSTUS	You want to make her out a wicked woman. She is not!
CECIL GRAHAM	Oh! Wicked women bother one. Good women bore one. That is the only difference between them.
LORD AUGUSTUS	[*Puffing a cigar.*] Mrs. Erlynne has a future before her.
DUMBY	Mrs. Erlynne has a past before her.
LORD AUGUSTUS	I prefer women with a past. They're always so demmed amusing to talk to.
CECIL GRAHAM	Well, you'll have lots of topics of conversation with HER, Tuppy. [*Rising and going to him.*]
LORD AUGUSTUS	You're getting annoying, dear-boy; you're getting demmed annoying.
CECIL GRAHAM	[*Puts his hands on his shoulders*.] Now, Tuppy, you've lost your figure and you've lost your character. Don't lose your temper; you have only got one.
LORD AUGUSTUS	My dear boy, if I wasn't the most good-natured man in London —
CECIL GRAHAM	We'd treat you with more respect, wouldn't we, Tuppy? [*Strolls away.*]
DUMBY	The youth of the present day are quite monstrous. They have absolutely no respect for dyed hair. [LORD AUGUSTUS *looks round angrily*.]
CECIL GRAHAM	Mrs. Erlynne has a very great respect for dear Tuppy.
DUMBY	Then Mrs. Erlynne sets an admirable example to the rest of her sex. It is perfectly brutal the way most women nowadays behave to men who are not their husbands.

Sources and Exam Questions

Text B — a conversation between teenage friends

A: mate you can't be serious

B: do I look like I'm joking (.) seriously he is

A: oh he is really not

B: come on no right (.) right he is though cos he's like

A: // he's proper minging

C: he is he's minging he is

B: // ah come on though I mean it's not like he is like compared to some people

A: compared to some people even more minging than him

B: well obviously compared to that right

A: // well then

B: // but that don't even make sense

C: why not

B: thing is though he's (2) okay thing is he's well fit

C: // [inaud]

B: // but he can be he can be well horrid sometimes

A: yeah right like (.) like exactly right I mean it's not like he's ever tret anyone good is it really

B: well I dunno (.) I dunno like he tret amanda quite good till she chucked him

A: she didn't dump

C: // it was him what got rid right (.) it was him what like got rid of her that's why why erm why she's

A: that's why she's such a mardy cow with him innit though right

B: // mardy cow that's

A: // yeah don't jip me right (3) no stop your giggling right she's well mardy with him

C: it's not like you can go blaming her for that though though (.) I mean bless her though cos fact of the matter is (.) fact is that she didn't do nowt wrong and he he he was he went behind her back and proper messed with her head (.) cos it was when she was supposed to meet him at pub (.) right she was gonna meet him at pub but he said he were doing summat else right so like (.) so like she goes anyway with her sister and he were there just like completely shameless with another bird

A: // no way

C: // yeah I mean bless her right (.) like she just don't deserve that

B: // soz defending amanda all of a sudden (.) I knew I knew

A: // it's dead obvious now though

C: what you trying to say

B: you'll not admit (.) he'll not admit to it like but you well fancy her

A: yep

C: whatever right (2) like I clearly don't but whatever if you wanna (.) wanna say

B: // yeah you do you've proper got hots for her

C: no way though we're just just (.) just get well and we just

B: // course yeah we're just good friends course (1) really good friends

A: yeah I don't (.) you'll not catch me snogging my friends (.) snogging

C: // what I ain't snogged her

Transcription Key

(.) *Micropause*

(2.0) *Pause in seconds*

// *Interruptions / overlapping speech*

[inaud] *An unidentified sound*

Sources and Exam Questions

Text C — an email between two employees at a company selling conservatories

RE: Guarantee query
Tony Craig
To: Jane Hilton

Hi Jane,

This was a common problem with the old gutter sleeve we were using at that time. There was a slant at the join with the abutment, which could cause the box gutter to come free and start to split.

If this was the problem in this case, then it's been usual practice in these circumstances to repair the gutter free of charge anyway as a goodwill gesture, because it's only minor.

You should be able to find most information like this in your I49 starting handbook, but if you have any more questions just give me a shout.

Tony

From: Jane Hilton
Sent: 04 August 2008 16:47
To: Tony Craig
Subject: Guarantee query

Hi Tony,

We've had a customer complaint about a uPVC Georgian Hip conservatory, fitted in 04/07.

We had to fit a box gutter because the roof slopes towards the fascia board. The gutter sleeve has now split and the customer wants it replacing under the two year guarantee.

Just wondering if the guarantee covers this?

Thanks

Jane

Text D — a restaurant review on the website gastronomyweb.com

I started with ham hock and parsley terrine, with a Cumberland sauce, confit onion and toasted sourdough — a really skilfully prepared dish and beautifully presented. My only complaint would be that the mountains of toasted sourdough meant that it was really far too big as a starter, and I had to leave about half a plateful.

With a selection of main courses including ballotine of chicken breast stuffed with spinach and ricotta, served with potato and beetroot gratin and sherry cream sauce; poached line-caught turbot and fresh tagliatelle, with fish velouté with lavender and Ossetra caviar; and their classic bouillabaisse, I really felt spoilt for choice. I opted for the ballotine of chicken breast, and wasn't disappointed. The tender chicken was perfectly complemented by earthy spinach and sweet, creamy ricotta.

Chef's take on sticky toffee pudding was disappointing — huge globs of pale pudding swimming in a sauce so ultra sweet that it completely dominated the palate. It didn't seem in keeping with the elegant, if robust, starter and delicate main — a little more gastropub than haute cuisine somehow. All was forgiven though when I tasted the hibiscus sorbet, which was a sharp and tangy triumph.

Service was prompt and attentive, but the staff seemed to feel the watchful eye of the steely maître d' enough to not hang around for long. The exception to this was the sommelier, who appeared to have very little to do and on one occasion had to be chivvied away from a table of pretty girls who were trying to get stuck into their moules marinières. On the whole, though, the chilliness of the maître d' was sufficiently warmed up by the coral walls, plush furnishings, and ultimately delicious food.

Sources and Exam Questions

Text E — a conversation between two mechanics (A and B) and a customer (C)

A: okay we've had a look and we couldn't pinpoint at first why it was (.) ah here's Greg actually it was Greg who was working on it mostly (.) erm I'll get him over (2.0) Greg

C: // okay

B: hiya (.) all right (1.0) back for the (.) er Range Rover is it (.) two point five diesel

C: yes that's right

A: I'm just saying it's you who was working on it really so do you (.) want to go through it and

B: // yeah yeah (.) no of course (.) great

C: great (.) thanks thank you

A: do you want to erm take him through to have a look at the v5 Greg

B: right yeah (.) yeah okay I'll get the get the v5 and we'll have a look

A: if you'd just like to come through here

C: // okay yes (.) okay

A: // we've had a bit of a problem with it really (.) the engine tone was changing slightly so we scanned it for any fault codes but we weren't getting anything from it

C: okay

A: so we thought it's like maybe (.) maybe your MAF playing up

C: // erm right (.) okay

A: // have you had any problems with that before

C: any problems with the (.) the sorry any problems with the (.) the erm (.) the (1.0) MAF

A: right no no (.) have you noticed any differences with your engine tone (2.0) sounds different (.) ever sound different

C: okay (.) erm no no (1.0) not re- (.) don't think I have really no

A: no problems in the past with that Greg

B: no (.) right no (.) I thought that but it can (.) it can just be it needs a clean (2.0) I mean I erm (.) I thought it was more that probably the injector was (.) yeah injector a bit blocked

A: // well yeah (.) that's what I'm thinking really (.) probably just your Injector being a bit blocked up (.) happens a lot with these models so it's

C: // yes (.) right yes okay (2.0) so what do you need to do with that (.) how will you fix it

A: basically what I'm thinking is that it's probably not a big problem

B: right yeah (.) not major like is it really

A: nothing major

C: // okay

A: just keep it in a bit longer so we can (.) I'll get Greg on it when (1.0) Greg when you've finished with that coupe (.) with the rev limiter on that coupe

B: // yeah cool (.) okay

A: // so if we get some Forté* in the fuel system then we'll see if that (.) I mean that could sort it completely (1.0) is that okay then

C: is that okay for (.) is that (.) erm yes no that should be fine (1.0) what I mean is I mean when do you think I can come and collect it

A: well Greg's got to finish this coupe (.) but then erm (.) well well it could be tomorrow morning I reckon

C: okay great (.) that's great (.) as long as you think that'll fix it (.) I really don't want to have to be coming back and forth again really if that's (.) it's just a bit of a pain when

A: // oh no worries yeah (.) yeah no a bit of Forté will do it

Forté™ is a brand of fuel treatment.

Language and Gender

Language and gender is a funny old game. There do seem to be some differences between how men and women use language, but no-one seems to be sure exactly what they are or why they occur. Here goes...

Men *and* Women *use* Language Differently

Studies have shown that women tend to use **accents** from a **higher social class** than men.

Her parents disapproved of her bit of rough, but Ange couldn't keep her hands off him.

- **Trudgill (1983)** studied men and women's **social class accents** (see p.32-35). He found that women's pronunciation was closer to **Received Pronunciation (RP)**, the accent that's usually seen as the most **prestigious**.
- **Cheshire (1982)** studied the speech of adolescent girls and boys, and found that boys tended to use more **non-standard grammatical forms**, e.g. *ain't*, than girls.

1) Using **Standard English** and **RP** gives a person **overt prestige** — the prestige of being associated with a respectable, well-off section of society. **Women** tend to seek **overt prestige** more than men.

2) Using **non-standard** English gives a person **covert prestige** — they seem a bit rebellious and independent. **Men** are more likely to seek **covert prestige** than women.

Women *may use more* Prestigious Forms *for* Several Reasons

There are several **possible explanations** for why **women** use more **prestigious** language than **men**.

1) Women might be **less secure** than men in terms of their **social status**. If they feel that they have an **inferior position** in society, then they might use more **prestigious** language to **overcome** it.

2) Society generally expects **higher standards** of **behaviour** from **women** — they're expected to behave like 'ladies' and use 'ladylike' language. This includes things like not swearing or arguing.

3) Men already have a **higher social status** than women, so they don't need to use prestigious forms to improve it. Instead, they seek **covert prestige** by using non-standard language that seems tough and rebellious.

4) **Non-standard language** is traditionally associated with **working-class** men, so men might use it to show that they share **traditionally masculine** qualities, like being '**tough**' and '**down-to-earth**'.

> Remember — these explanations are based on studies of a few men and women. You can't generalise them to all men and women. There have also been changes in gender roles since the 1980s, when these studies were done.

Women's *language is usually* More Polite *than* Men's

The researcher **Robin Lakoff (1975)** identified features that she felt were characteristic of women's language:

> **Hedges and fillers** — fragments of language like *sort of, kind of, maybe*.
> **Apologetic requests** — e.g. *I'm **sorry**, but **would you mind** closing the door?*
> **Tag questions** — e.g. *this is nice, **isn't it?***
> **Indirect requests** — e.g. *It's very noisy out there* (meaning — *could you close the door?*)

1) **Lakoff** also pointed out that women tend to **speak less** than men, use **fewer expletives** (swear less), and use more **intensifiers** (words like **so** and **very**).

2) She argued that these features of women's language reflected women's **inferior social status**, and made it worse by making them seem **indecisive** and **needy**. She said that women's language is **weak** compared to men's language, and this **prevents** women from being **taken seriously**. This explanation is known as the **deficit model**.

3) **O'Barr and Atkins (1980)** suggested an alternative explanation to the **deficit model**. They analysed transcripts of **American courtroom trials**. They found that **male and female** witnesses who were of **low social status** and/or inexperienced with the courtroom practices, both showed many of the linguistic features that Lakoff labelled **female**.

4) This suggests that the kind of language **Lakoff** describes as female isn't only found in women, and might be more to do with individuals feeling **powerless**.

> **Lakoff's** research is quite **old**. More recently, researchers like **Holmes (1984)** have suggested that 'women's language' doesn't show **weakness**, but a desire to **co-operate**. Linguists like **Cameron (2007)** argue that there are actually very **few differences** between men and women's language, and **situation** affects how people speak much more than **gender**.

Language and Gender

Language can be Explained in terms of Dominance and Difference

Linguists have come up with other models to explain the **differences** between men and women's language.

1) Dominance model

- **Zimmerman and West (1975)** recorded interruptions in conversations between men and women.
- They found that **96%** of the interruptions were by men.
- This suggested that men are **dominant** in **male-female conversations**. They argued that this reflects male dominance in society.

2) Difference model

Tannen (1990) described male and female conversational style in terms of **difference**.

- **Men** are concerned with **status** and **independence**, e.g. they interrupt a lot.
- They give **direct orders**, e.g. *pass me that*, and don't mind **conflict**.
- **Men** are interested in gaining **factual information** and finding **solutions to problems**.

- **Women** are interested in **forming bonds** — they tend to talk less and agree more than men.
- They usually give polite, indirect orders, e.g. *would you mind passing me that*, and try to **avoid conflict**.
- **Women** aim to show **understanding** by **compromising**, and offering **support** rather than **solutions**.

The **reasons** for these **differences** in male and female interaction could be to do with the **topics** that they talk about in **single sex groups**, e.g. traditionally **male** topics of conversation have focused on **work** and **sport**, where **factual information** and **status** are important. Traditionally **female** topics have centred on the **home** and **family**, where **emotions**, **support** and **compassion** are important.

There are Problems with these Explanations

Other researchers have cast **doubts** on some of these explanations of differences in **male** and **female language**.

1) **Beattie (1982)** questioned **Zimmerman and West's** idea that men **interrupting** women was a sign of **dominance**. He suggested that interruptions can be **supportive** and show that the person is listening, e.g. if they **repeat** what the speaker is saying, or say things like *yes* and *mm*.

2) **Cameron (2007)** argues that a lot of research is **biased** because there has been more focus on the **differences** between male and female language, which are actually quite small, rather than the **similarities**.

Practice Questions

Q1 What is meant by the terms overt prestige and covert prestige?
Q2 List the main features Lakoff attributed to female language.
Q3 Why might 'powerless language' be a better term to use than 'women's language'?
Q4 Explain the dominance model.
Q5 List the main features of Tannen's analysis of male and female language.

Essay Question

Q1 Outline the differences in the way that men and women use language. Explain some of the reasons for these differences.

To make your essay more balanced, you could focus on the different explanations that researchers have offered, as well as the problems with some of these explanations.

Try to avoid making genderalisations...

A lot of the stuff people believe about men and women's speech is based on stereotypes about what they think men and women are like. It's possible to think of loads of exceptions to any of these 'rules', and yet still assume that they must be true. Just remember, the way people speak is affected by loads of different factors, and gender is only one of them...

Language and Gender

These pages are about the different ways that men and women are spoken and written about in things like adverts, fiction and non-fiction. The basic idea is that the way they're represented shapes how men and women are perceived.

Men and Women are Represented Differently

1) **Sexist language** is language that **insults**, **patronises** or **ignores** people on the basis of their **gender**.
2) There is a lot **more** sexist language about **women** than men.
3) Some language implies that the **male** version is the **norm**, and the **female** version is **different** or **wrong**:

Marked terms
- These are words that reveal a person's **gender**, e.g. *policeman*, *wife*.
- **Unmarked terms** don't reveal the person's gender, e.g. *police officer*, *spouse*.
- Some words are **marked** by a **feminising suffix**, e.g. *actress, usherette, comedienne*.
  The suffix implies that the male version is the **original** or the **norm**, so it seems **superior** to the female version.

Generic terms
- This is when a **marked term** is used to refer to both men and women.
- It's nearly always **masculine terms** which are used to mean **people** in general, rather than just **men**.
- The most common example is the word *man*, e.g. the noun *mankind*, or the verb in *to **man** the desk*.
- **Generic terms** refer to everybody, but using them can make **females** seem **invisible** by **ignoring** them. When this occurs, women are said to be occupying **negative semantic space**.

Lexical Asymmetry refers to **pairs of words** that appear to have a **similar meaning**, but aren't **equally balanced**, e.g. *bachelor* and *spinster* (unmarried men and women).
- The connotations of *bachelor* are usually **positive** — it's associated with a man living a care-free, independent life.
- The connotations of *spinster* are usually **negative** — it implies that the woman has been unable to find a partner.

Patronising terms are words used by speakers that imply **superiority** over the person they're talking to.
- Terms that imply someone is **younger** than the speaker can be patronising, e.g. *girls, young lady*.
- **Terms of endearment** can be **patronising** in some circumstances, e.g. *love, dear, sweetheart*.
- Whether a word is **patronising** depends on the **context**, e.g. a male employee who addresses a female colleague as *love* could be seen as patronising, but boyfriends and girlfriends calling each other *love* might not.

Grammar can be Sexist

The idea that the **male** is the **norm** is also evident in English **grammar**.

1) **Pronouns** — the 3rd person masculine pronoun *he* or *his* is often used to refer to both men and women, e.g. ***an employee** who is absent for longer than five days must obtain a sick note from **his** doctor*.
2) **Syntax** — when one gender specific word is always placed before another, it's known as **order of preference**, e.g. *Mr and Mrs, men and women, Sir or Madam*. Usually the male term comes first.

There are More Insults for Women than Men

There seem to be a lot **more insulting terms** for **women** than there are for **men**. This is known as **over-representation**.
1) Lots of insulting terms for **women** have an **animal** theme, e.g. *bitch, cow*.
2) There are lots of words to label women as **promiscuous**, e.g. *slag, slut, slapper*.
3) There are hardly any **equivalents** for men. Terms like *stud* tend to have **positive connotations**. Terms like *man whore* or *male slut* tend to be used **comically**, and imply that the **female** version is the **norm**.
4) The **lack** of an **equivalent term** for something — e.g. a male term for *slut* — is known as a **lexical gap**.

Language and Gender

Sexist Language can be Avoided and Changed

1) The **Sex Discrimination Act** was passed in **1975** to **protect** people from sexual discrimination and harassment, especially at work and at school.

2) It reflected the work of **feminist campaigners**, who wanted to promote **equality** between men and women.

3) Part of this campaign was a push to get rid of **sexist language**.

4) The idea is that language doesn't just **reflect** sexist **attitudes** — it helps to **keep them alive**.

5) So if you change **discriminatory language**, then people's **attitudes** might change too.

6) This is often called **political correctness** (more on this on p.53).

7) **Sexist terms** can be avoided by **replacing** them with **gender neutral** ones.

The only surefire way to remove gender issues... get everyone to dress like an idiot.

For example...

1) **Marked terms** can be replaced with **unmarked terms**, e.g. *head teacher* instead of *headmaster* or *headmistress*, *police officer* instead of *policeman* or *policewoman*.

2) **Feminising suffixes** can be **dropped**, e.g. a female manager is called a *manager*, not a *manageress*.

3) Instead of *Mrs* or *Miss*, the title *Ms* is often used, so you **can't tell** whether a woman is **married**.

4) The generic use of **man** can be replaced by gender neutral terms, e.g. *humankind* instead of *mankind*, *workforce* instead of *manpower*.

5) The **generic** use of the masculine 3rd person pronoun (*he*) can be replaced by *he/she*, *s/he*, or *they*. Sentences can be made **gender-neutral** by using the **plural** instead, e.g. ***Employees*** *who are absent for longer than five days must obtain a sick note from **their** doctor.*

People have Different Views about Avoiding Sexist Language

1) The point of encouraging people to avoid sexist language is to ensure people will be treated **equally**, and not feel they're being **singled out**, or **ignored**, because of their gender.

2) Sometimes there are **problems** with trying to **control language** in this way. People can feel that it's **controlling**, and find it frustrating because they feel they can't speak their minds without getting into trouble. Some people argue that this can create **resentment** towards the group of people it's designed to protect.

3) It's hard to **enforce** the use of non-sexist language. Some people think that condemning all sexist language ignores **context** and **intent**, e.g. if everyone understands that a comment is a joke, and nobody is offended by it, then it's **pointless** to have laws that stop people from making it.

Practice Questions

Q1 Outline what is meant by the term negative semantic space.
Q2 Explain the term lexical asymmetry and provide two examples.
Q3 What is meant by the term lexical gap?
Q4 Outline three ways in which sexist language can be avoided.
Q5 Explain one argument for and one argument against changing language to avoid sexism.

Essay Question

Q1 How can language be used to suggest that women are inferior to men?

I'm not sexist — some of my best friends are men or women...

This is one of those topics where it can feel like you're stating the obvious some of the time, but at least it's not really complicated. And it's a good one for having a bit of a debate over as well. Just remember that you have to show you understand both sides of an argument before you start waving placards and holding a sit-in in the exam hall...

Language and Power

There are loads of ways to assert power over someone in a conversation — when stuffing your fist into the other person's mouth isn't an option, try some of these strategies instead...

The **Language** of **Power** is found in **Different Contexts**

The language of **power** tries to exert **influence** or **control**. It appears in various **contexts**, and in both spoken and written forms.

1) Political language

The purpose of political language is to **persuade**. To achieve this, politicians use **rhetorical devices** (**rhetoric** is the **art** of using language **persuasively**).

1) **Repetition** — *Those who **betray** their party **betray** themselves.*

2) **Three-part lists** — *He came, he saw, he conquered.*

3) **First person plural pronoun** (*we*) — *__We__ must strive together for the better health of the nation.*

4) **Figurative language** — *Under our leadership, the **winter of discontent** has become a **summer of prosperity**.*

5) **Rhetorical questions** — *How much longer must our people endure this injustice?*

6) **Hyperbole** (exaggeration) — *Plague would be a better option than the health policies proposed.*

2) Legal language

1) **Legal language** is quite distinctive — it has its own **lexis**. The specific vocabulary used by an **occupational group** is know as **jargon** (see p.40-41 and p.52).

2) The syntax is often **complex**, with lots of **subordinate clauses**. It's also **repetitive**.

3) Because it's so complex, knowledge of this language gives **specialists** a distinct **advantage** over **non-specialists**. This means that lawyers have a lot of **power** — if their clients don't fully understand the difficult jargon, then they have to **trust** that their lawyers understand it and will deal with their case properly.

3) Education

1) The language of power is seen in schools, colleges and universities. The language of **education** reflects the **power structures** in schools.

2) Teachers often use **imperatives** — *open your books*, and direct questions — *what's the answer to question four?*

3) Students use **fewer imperatives** and ask more **indirect questions** — *is it okay if I go to the toilet?*

4) There's often an **imbalance** in **address terms** — students might use respectful address terms to the teacher like **Sir**, or **title + surname** constructions (Ms Smith), while teachers just use the student's **first name**. This shows an **understanding** that the teacher has **authority**.

4) Business

1) **Power structures** in the language of **business** are very similar to those in **education** — **managers** may speak more **directly** to their **employees**, while **employees** may use more **politeness strategies** (see p.27) and fewer **imperatives**.

2) The hierarchical structure of many businesses is shown in nouns such as **subordinate**, **superior**, **team leader** and **chief executive**.

Address Terms show Power Relationships

What people **call** each other can reveal **power relationships**. As with everything, they **vary** in different **contexts**.

Context	Form of Address
Politics	*Madam/Mr Speaker, Honourable Member*
Law	*Your Honour, Ladies and Gentlemen of the Jury*
Education	*Sir, Miss, Mr Briggs, Ms Briggs, Dr / Professor*
Business	*Madam Chair, Sir, Madam*

Look out for **imbalances** in address terms, because they can reveal **unequal power relationships**.

Language and Power

There are Different Ways to Exert Power in a Conversation

Power relationships are shown in the way people talk to each other. People **assert** power in different ways.

1) **Initiating a conversation** — this can be a means of **taking the lead** and establishing the **topic** of conversation.

2) **Holding the floor** — this is when one speaker gives little or no opportunity for other speakers to take a turn. Usually conversation involves **turn-taking**, so a speaker can show **dominance** by not letting anyone else in.

3) **Imperative sentences** — giving **orders** and **directions** can be a sign of **dominance**, e.g. *shut the door.*

4) **Interrupting** — some **interruptions** cut into the other person's turn. It shows that the person interrupting has **little interest** in what the speaker is saying.

5) **Unresponsiveness** — this a more **negative** way of asserting control. If the person speaking is ignored or if the **back-channel noises** (*mm* or *uh huh*) of the other participants are half-hearted or hesitant then the **status** of the speaker is **undermined**.

6) **Questioning** — questions direct the **topic** of conversation, and make it clear when the other person is **expected** to talk.

7) **Topic changing** — this can be a technique of **reasserting control**. Sometimes politicians do this when they're uncomfortable talking about a particular topic. By **diverting attention** to a **different topic**, where they may have something more positive to say, they're trying to **gain control** over the **direction** of the conversation.

8) **Closing down a conversation** — this asserts power by not allowing other speakers to carry on talking, e.g. saying *goodbye* or walking away.

Context is Important

It's important to pay attention to the **context** of a conversation when you're looking at **power**.

1) In a particular **situation**, the way power shows itself depends on how people are '**positioned**' in relation to each other.

2) These **relationships** between speakers can **shape** the **conversational strategies** and **type** of language they use, e.g. you'd **expect** a doctor to ask a patient lots of questions.

3) Depending on the context of the conversation, some of the above examples of **dominance** can actually be interpreted as ways of showing **support**.

4) For example, **interrupting** with words like *yes*, or cutting in to **repeat** what the speaker has said can show that you **agree** and you're **listening**. It doesn't necessarily mean that you're trying to assert power over the person speaking.

5) Similarly, **asking questions** can be a sign you want to **control** the topic of conversation, **or** it can be a way of **passing control** to somebody else to **encourage** them to **hold the floor**.

Practice Questions

Q1 What is rhetoric and what are rhetorical devices?

Q2 Why might a teacher prefer to be addressed by title + surname rather than by first name?

Q3 Outline three ways in which a speaker might try to dominate a conversation.

Essay Question

A: it's so funny isn't it darling (1) do you like it (.) it's really clever and //
B: // but it's so unrealistic turn it off
A: you can't say that (.) you've only just seen a bit of it
B: I don't need to realise (.) to see how bad it is (2) it's like //
A: // fine (1) just put something else on

Q1 How do the speakers in this extract exert power over each other?

Forget language — just get down the gym and show 'em who's boss...

This is a handy little topic — you can find evidence of language and power in pretty much any extract you'll have to look at. There are loads of different ways to exert power, so you shouldn't get too bored. Personally, when I want to dominate a conversation I go for the good old-fashioned fingers-in-ears-la-la-la-I'm-not-listening-to-you technique. Works every time...

Language and Power

The language of power is about dominating your enemies and crushing your opponents, so they cower at your mighty presence and quiver in the face of your wrath. Mwahahaha...

Power *shows itself in* Different Ways

The ways people **exert power** in a conversation aren't just about what they say.

1) **Non-verbal communication** (**NVC**) is using **posture, positioning, gestures, eye contact** and **facial expressions** to convey feelings and attitudes, e.g. crossing your legs away from someone can function as a **barrier** and appear **defensive**. Maintaining eye contact longer than normal can be an attempt to **assert dominance**. **Smiling** at someone and **pausing** as you walk past them can be a way of **initiating conversation**.

2) **Non-verbal aspects of speech** (**pitch, intonation, volume, pace** and **stress**) can also be used to assert control, e.g. when people **argue** they may try to dominate by **shouting**, raising the **pitch** of their voice or speaking more **quickly**.

3) **Standard English** and **Received Pronunciation** (**RP**) (see p.34-35) are the varieties of English that carry the most **prestige**. They're associated with **professional jobs** and a **good education**. Because of this, speakers who use Standard English and RP are often perceived to have more **authority** and **status** than people who speak in a regional dialect or accent.

Bruce didn't need words — he had raw animal strength.

Jargon *can be used to* Dominate

Jargon is the **specialist vocabulary** used in particular **fields** of **activity**, especially **occupations** (see p.40-41). For example

- The **medical world** uses terms like *adenovirus, meningococcal,* and *septum.*
- **Electrical engineers** use terms like *chrominance, phase jitter,* and *watchdog circuit.*
- Terms like these aren't generally understood by **non-specialists**.

1) **Jargon** is often **necessary** when **specialists** are talking to **other specialists** — it's a **precise** form of **labelling** objects, processes and conditions, so it means **technical information** can be communicated **quickly**.

2) People who **understand** the jargon have a sense of **inclusion** in a group, which often brings a **higher status**.

3) The **problem** with jargon is that when **specialists** use it to communicate with **non-specialists** it can become a **barrier** to **understanding**, e.g. doctors with patients, mechanics with car owners.

4) **Non-specialists** can feel **intimidated** by the **specialists** and **excluded** from the **high-status group**. In cases like this, the **specialists** have more power and can **dominate** the situation.

5) **Specialists** can exploit this by using jargon with **non-specialists** in order to **impress** them — it makes people feel that they want to be **part** of the high-status group that uses such specialist terms. It can also be used to hide what's really going on.

There are Alternatives *to using* Jargon

Jargon can cause real **problems** when it's used **inappropriately**, so different measures are taken to avoid it. For example:

1) Since 1999 some of the language used in the **civil courts** has been changed to make it easier for non-specialists to understand.

2) This includes **Latin** terms like *in camera* and *subpoena*, which have been replaced by *in private* and *witness summons*.

3) Using plainer language promotes **equality**, because it means that everyone has more chance of understanding what's being said, and specialists can't use jargon to **intimidate** non-specialists.

- The **Plain English Campaign** was set up in 1979 to **combat** the use of **confusing** and **unnecessary jargon**.
- It **advises organisations** on how they can use **plainer language**.
- Organisations can apply for the **Crystal Mark**, which shows that the **Plain English Campaign** has approved their documents.

Language and Power

Political Correctness aims to Promote Equality

1) Political correctness is a term to describe ways that language can be adapted to **minimise social inequality**.

2) It's politically correct to avoid language that **insults**, **marginalises** or seeks to **control** other people or groups of people — in particular language that is **sexist**, **racist**, **ageist** and **ableist** (discriminates against people with disabilities).

3) Political correctness is based on the idea that language doesn't just **reflect** social attitudes, but also helps to **shape** them. So if discriminatory language is changed or avoided, then people are less likely to discriminate against others.

There are always **reasons why** terms are viewed as **politically incorrect**, e.g.

Original term	Alternative	Reason
half caste	mixed race	*half caste* suggests less than whole, incomplete.
stewardess	flight attendant	*stewardess* reveals the person's gender. The suffix **-ess** suggests that the male term (*steward*) is the original, so more important.
disabled person	person with disabilities	*disabled person* is a dehumanising label — it characterises people by their disability. The alternative version takes the focus away from the disability.

There's a lot of Debate about Political Correctness

Arguments for Political Correctness

- Language helps to **shape social attitudes**. Changing it sends a clear message about what is **acceptable**, which encourages people to change their attitudes.

- It acts as a **symbol** that society is committed to becoming more **equal** and **inclusive**.

- It's often **blown out of proportion** — people focus on **outrageous** examples of political correctness, when most actually have a **reasonable explanation**.

Arguments against Political Correctness

- People feel they're being **restricted**, and can't speak their minds without getting into trouble.

- It's pointless because language only **reflects** social **attitudes**, it **doesn't shape** them.

- Some feel it creates **resentment** towards the groups it tries to protect, so discrimination is just as likely.

- It's pointless because language **always changes** — words that **were** once politically correct eventually become **less acceptable**. For example, *Third World* was replaced by *Developing World*, but now *Majority World* or *Less Economically Developed Country* (*LEDC*) is seen as more politically correct.

Practice Questions

Q1 Give some examples of jargon associated with medicine.

Q2 In what ways can jargon be seen as a positive use of language?

Q3 How is jargon sometimes misused?

Q4 In what way might political correctness be a good thing?

Q5 Why do some people argue against political correctness?

Essay Question

Q1 Outline some of the ways that people can use communication to exert power over each other, and discuss whether it's important to change the language to avoid this.

You could focus especially on the use of jargon, and debates about political correctness.

It's political correctness gone mad...

This stuff is gold, and that's scientific fact. Talking about non-verbal communication might seem a bit weird, but it can be really useful — if you get an extract from some fiction, and it describes a speaker sighing or gesticulating or whatever, then just whack in something about NVC and the marks are yours. Gesticulate. Tee hee hee. Sounds a bit rude somehow...

Language and Power

These pages are about language and power in terms of the media. Sounds tricky, but it's basically just how the language of things like newspapers, magazines, TV, adverts, radio, the Internet and films can be used to persuade the audience.

The **Media** holds **Considerable Power**

The language of the media can have a big influence on people's **attitudes** and **values**. This occurs in a number of ways.

1) **Bias** — the tendency to **take sides** and view things **subjectively**, e.g. only focusing on the positive aspect of a new law or political party, or using **loaded** and **emotive** language to present factual information, e.g. *tragic*.

2) **Prejudice** — a **preconceived** opinion of a person or group that isn't based on **experience** or **reason**. Media texts can **create** and **reinforce** these negative opinions so that an audience begin to associate them with a particular group of people, e.g. describing asylum seekers as *scrounging from the taxpayer*.

3) **Stereotypes** — **simplified** images or descriptions of people and events. The most common are based around **gender roles**, in which men are viewed in a certain way, and women in another (see p.48-49). The media can easily **create** and **reinforce** stereotypes when presenting pictures, information and opinions.

4) The media can also affect an audience's **point of view** by **sensationalising** stories (making a big deal out of them), being **selective** with quotes or information, or using **ambiguous** language.

Adverts are the most **Persuasive** form of media

All adverts aim to **attract** an audience to a particular product, service or cause, by focusing on the following things.

1) **Selling** — advert makers use different approaches to do this, e.g. showing **attractive people** with **luxurious lifestyles** using a product to persuade the audience to buy it.

2) **Form** — written adverts come in different forms, e.g. in newspapers and magazines. They can also be in the form of appeal letters that come through your door, leaflets, posters and e-mails (SPAM).

3) The **target audience** is the audience the advert is aimed at. This could be very **broad** (food shoppers, drivers) or more **specific** (boys who like snowboarding).

4) The **hook** is the device advertisers use to get the audience's attention — it could be **verbal**, **visual** or **musical**.

5) In paper-based adverts the **text** is referred to as **copy**. People who **write** adverts are sometimes called **copywriters**. It's their job to come up with ways to make adverts interesting and grab their target audience's attention.

Adverts use a number of **Creative Features**

1) Adverts **manipulate** language just like any other **persuasive** text. Here are a few examples.

- **Lexis** — comparative and superlative **adjectives** and hi-tech **jargon** make the product seem state-of-the-art.
- **Grammar** — imperatives without subjects are common **hooks**, e.g. *unite*, *enjoy*, but adverts use all kinds of sentence functions. They also use **disjunctive** sentences (e.g. *elegant but sturdy*) to make **concise comparisons**.
- **Phonology** — adverts often rely on **alliteration**, **onomatopoeia** and **rhyme** to make them unique and **appealing**.
- **Graphology** — the images, colour and typeface are also carefully chosen to make the advert **stand out**.
- **Discourse structure** — the **hook** is normally followed by further **persuasion** or **information**, and then **instructions** on how to get hold of the product, e.g. price, where it's available, how to contact the company, etc.

2) Using **puns** and well-known **collocations** also grabs the audience's **attention**, and sticks in their minds.

- **Semantic puns**, e.g. *Fly with us, the sky's the limit.*
- **Phonetic puns**, e.g. *Hair today, gone tomorrow.*
- **Figurative language**, e.g. *Is there a black hole in your pocket? Start saving now!*

3) Referencing other texts is called **intertextuality**. This can create a more memorable and **accessible** text.

- For example, a **hook** for a mattress advert — *and on the seventh day he rested*. This echoes words from the Bible, so a lot of people will recognise it. This is aimed at quite a general **target audience**.
- Other adverts aim to appeal to a more **specific** audience. They reference lesser-known texts to 'stroke' the audience — they will feel knowledgeable and know that the product will only appeal to an **elite few**.
- E.g. a **hook** for a luxury travel company advertising city breaks in London and Paris — *A Tale of Two Cities*. This references the title of a Charles Dickens novel, which not everyone would be familiar with.

Language and Power

Tabloid Newspapers use Different Language to Broadsheets

Every newspaper takes a slightly **different political viewpoint**, so their purpose is to **persuade** as well as to **inform**. Newspapers are in **competition** with each other, so they also need to **entertain** readers to keep them interested.

1) **Tabloid newspapers** are ones like *The Sun* and *The News of the World*. They tend to make their viewpoint on a story very clear, and use quite **straightforward language**.

2) **Broadsheets** are newspapers such as *The Guardian* and *The Daily Telegraph*. They're aimed at a **professional**, mostly **middle class readership**.

Features of tabloid newspapers	Features of broadsheet newspapers
Short paragraphs	**Longer** paragraphs
Large font, spread out	**Smaller font**, compact
Large print, sensational headlines (*May Day Massacre*)	**Smaller print**, factual headlines (*PM Defeat at Polls*)
Lots of **large photographs**	Fewer, **smaller photographs**
Short, Anglo-Saxon words (*think, dead*)	**Long, Latinate** words (*cogitate, deceased*)
Simple sentences with few clauses	**Complex sentences** with more **subordinate** clauses
Simple punctuation, exclamation marks	**Complex punctuation**, few exclamation marks
First names or **nicknames** (*Gordon, Macca*)	**Full names** or **surnames** (*Gordon Brown, McCartney*)
Sensationalised news stories, **one-sided** point of view	**Fact-based** news stories, often more **objective** stance
Emotive vocabulary (*Monster rapist gets off with five years*)	**Neutral** vocabulary (*Rapist gets five year sentence*)
Personalisation	**Impersonal** tone
Informal vocabulary (*pal, kids*)	More **formal** vocabulary (*friend, children*)
Use of **phonological features** like alliteration and rhyme. Also **phonetic spelling** (*No Bovver Says Becks*)	Fewer **phonological features** (*No Problem for Beckham*)
Use of **puns** (*Santa's Grotty*)	**Few** puns

1) Newspaper language also makes use of **modifier + headword** constructions.

2) In the case of **tabloids** this is often for **sensational effect**, e.g. emotive modifiers such as *tragic* hero, *incest* fiend, *heartbroken* midfielder, *chilling* image.

3) **Broadsheets** use these constructions less. When they do, they tend to be more factual, e.g. *experienced* manager, *Dublin-born* criminal. For a direct comparison, see p.14.

Practice Questions

Q1 What is prejudice? Give a linguistic example.
Q2 Explain the terms target audience, hook, and copy.
Q3 Describe how adverts use lexis, grammar, phonology and graphology to appeal to their audience.
Q4 Outline three main differences between tabloid and broadsheet newspapers.
Q5 What is the effect of modifer + headword constructions?

Essay Question

Q1 Compare and contrast these two headlines:

More Cash For Single Mum Scroungers   Single Mothers Can Claim More Benefits

ENG LANG STUDENT IN NAP ON DESK SHOCKER...

It's at about this stage that the mind starts wandering — like, how many newspapers would it take to wrap up every surface you could see... Yes it might be a fire hazard, yes it might go soggy when it rains, yes the ink might rub off on your face when you go to bed (details, details). Don't listen to the naysayers. Join me, and together we shall paper the world with news.

Language and Technology

Technology has a huge impact on language. As new things are invented, new words are needed to describe them — proof if ever you need it that life without TV or the Internet really would be boring and utterly pointless...

Radio Language is Different to TV Language

1) **TV language** has the support of **pictures**, **gestures** and **facial expressions**, and sometimes **text**.

2) On the **radio** there aren't any visual clues, so listeners have to rely on **what** speakers say and **how** they say it.

3) This affects the **type** of language used in each medium. For example:

Radio commentary of a football match

here's Burton making space along the left hand side (1.0) Peters in support to his right (2.0) cross hit hard and low (.) Oliver picks it up on the far right side by the corner flag (.) cuts inside (.) passes to Hilton

Linguistic features
- Lots of information.
- Full sentences.
- Lots of adjectives (e.g. — *hard*, *low*).
- Short pauses.

The numbers in brackets indicate the length of pauses in seconds.

TV commentary of a football match

here's Burton (4.0) Burton's cross (2.0) Oliver (3.0)

Linguistic features
- Minimal information.
- Incomplete sentences.
- Long pauses.

Telephone Language is Dialogue

1) Telephone language shares many features with **face-to-face dialogue**. This includes **non-fluency features**, like **fillers** and **false starts**, and **non-verbal** aspects of speech, like **intonation** and **stress**.

2) The **opening sequence** is very formulaic, and generally involves the same **adjacency pairs** — the person answering says **hello**, and the person phoning says **who they are** or who they **wish to speak to**. Differences in this sequence usually depend on the **age** of the speaker — **older** people are more likely to answer with something like *Molesey 326*, while **younger** people tend to be **less formal**, e.g. *All right, Tyler*. How you answer can also depend on **context**, e.g. people tend to be more **formal** at **work** than at **home**.

3) **Mobile phones** are an exception to this. You can usually **see who's calling** before you answer, and the person phoning can be more certain of who's going to pick up, so the opening sequence is more **flexible** and **casual**.

4) The lack of **non-verbal communication** means that telephone language includes quite **strict turn-taking**, because there are no **visual clues** to indicate when a speaker has finished. There are also **few pauses**.

Mobile Phones have had a Big Impact on Language

Probably the biggest influence that mobile phones have had on language is **text speak**.

1) Text messaging is **creative** — it's not **standardised**, so everyone uses it slightly differently. It's a **mixed mode** of communication, because it's a **written** language that contains many features of **spoken** language (see p.31).

2) These distinctive features have come about because of a need to **communicate quickly**. Typing complete words into a mobile phone keypad is time-consuming, so text speak has evolved as a form of **shorthand**.

Feature	Example
acronyms	LOL (Laugh Out Loud)
numbers for words	2 (to)
numbers for phonemes (sounds)	gr8 (great)
symbols for words	@ (at)
phonetic spelling	coz (because)
incomplete clauses	home safe. speak soon
no punctuation	how u doin wana go out 2nite
simple sentences	went to the zoo. it was good.
smileys / emoticons	:-)

Roger hadn't quite got the hang of this texting lark.

Language and Technology

The *Internet* has affected language too

The language used over the internet, e.g. in **e-mail**, **live chat** and **forums,** shares some of the linguistic features of mobile text messaging.

1) E-mails are a **mixed mode**, containing **spoken** and **written** features. The mode that dominates depends on how **formal** the email is.

2) Internet language is dependent on **context**. An e-mail from one business to another business might be set out like a **formal letter** and use **Standard English** (p.34-35). But friends communicating in a chatroom might use **text speak**, and language normally associated with **informal spoken** English — e.g. **slang**, **non-standard grammar**.

3) Internet communication involves certain **conventions**, known as **netiquette**. This includes things like avoiding using all **capital letters**, because this is the equivalent of shouting.

New technology can be baffling.

New Technology has Created New Words and Meanings

Every piece of new technology needs **new words** to describe it. This can involve giving **existing** words **new meanings**, or **inventing** completely new terms.

Way of forming new words	Example
acronyms — the initial letters from a group of words form a new word	radar (**ra**dio **d**etection **and r**anging)
affixation — adding a prefix or suffix to an existing word	**hyper**text
compounding — combining separate words	webcrawler, spyware
clipping — a shortened word becomes a word in its own right	fax (from facsimile)
blending — parts of two words are combined	netizen (net + citizen)
conversion — an existing word changes its grammatical function	**the text** (noun) becomes **to text** (verb)

TV also increases people's knowledge of **specialist vocabulary** from **different fields**. Documentaries and the news do this to a certain extent, but programmes about specific occupations also have an impact, e.g. **medical dramas**, **courtroom dramas** and **cop shows**.

Practice Questions

Q1 What is the basic difference between TV and radio and what impact can this have on language use?

Q2 Outline one difference between telephone dialogue and face-to-face dialogue.

Q3 How does text speak differ from standard written English?

Q4 Define each of the following methods of forming new words: affixation, compounding, conversion.

Essay Question

Hey Sweetie!
hows you? what's my favourite sis been up2 — haven't heard from u in AGES, grrrr!! Anyway ive got some dead dead excitin news... I found a photo of you from when ur little in the bath and im gonna post it on the net for all to see... Nah not really lol! Actually, heard that Pat's comin back from australia next month! See, i knew ud be excited! Well, got to go, but see you really soon for a catch up — gimme a text next time ur free xxoxx

Q1 This is an extract of an email an 18 year old girl sent to her sister.
Analyse it in terms of the impact that technology has had on the language.

This was all fields in my day...

If you get an extract from anything that's got even the merest sniff of technology about it, then throw in this stuff and you're laughing. See, it's not such a bad life really — pretty much everyone watches TV and knows about texting, but not everyone gets to talk about it in their exams. Just don't try to do any actual texting in your exams though — it won't go down well.

Sources and Exam Questions

Here are some exam-style questions, with sources like the ones you'll get in the real paper.

> 1. The text below is a transcript of a conversation between the manager of a shoe shop and two trainees. It is their first day.
>
>   What is the significance of gender in this interaction?　　　*[48 marks]*

M: right Josh I want you to work in the men's section (.) is that okay

J: cool

M: and you Susie erm I'd like you to man the customer service desk at first (.) that's on the lower floor (.) okay with that

S: yes (.) yes (.) that's fine

M: great (.) now then (.) let me tell what I'll (.) what I'll expect from you

S: mm mm

M: ok you need to be here by eight-thirty every morning (1.0) and I mean eight-thirty yes

J: sure

S: yes but erm er (1.0) sometimes (.) sorry I hope it's okay but my bus is late sometimes so (.) it should be fine

M: no that's okay (.) but if you can see about getting an earlier one if you can

S: mm mm no of course (.) sorry

M: there's not always much you do about it though is there (.) don't worry sweetheart (2.0) now

J:　　　　　　　　　　　　　　　　　　　　　　　　　　　　// I live near yours Suzie

S: okay (.) erm

J: I'll give you a lift

S: oh are you sure (1.0) if you're sure that'd be great (.) thank you

M: brilliant (.) good lad (1.0) that's that sorted then (.) okay erm breaktimes for you two are erm ten forty-five to eleven (.) in the morning erm and two forty-five to three in the afternoon (2.0) finish at five

J: what about lunch-time

M: good question (1.0) lunchtime (1.0) we don't want a growing lad like you starving now do we (1.0) one till two (1.0) right (1.0) everything clear

S: yes thank you (.) although I just wondered

J:　　　　　　　　　　// fine (1.0) do we work every Saturday

M: no (.) alternate Saturdays erm we'll need to work out which ones I er want you in for later (2.0) but we'll do that later (.) now (1) the till

J:　　　　　　　　　　　　// don't worry about me (.) I were on the tills in me last job

M: great (.) okay what about you Suzie

S: yep no that's fine (.) I've worked in shops before

M: right (2.0) little miss efficient eh

S: mm

M: okay so we'll have Josh (.) you on the tills at first right (2.0) so Susie (1.0) polite at all times (2.0) and don't forget to smile (1.0) you going to be OK with that Susie

S: yep think so (1.0) thanks (.) can I ask for help if I need it

J: cool

Transcription Key

(.) — *brief pause*

(3.0) — *Numbers within brackets indicate length of pause in seconds*

// — *interruption or overlapping speech*

M — Manager

S — Female Trainee

J — Male Trainee

Sources and Exam Questions

2. The text below is a transcript of part of a Chemistry lesson.

What do you observe about the power relationships in this extract?   *[48 marks]*

T — Teacher
A, B, C, D — Pupils

T: settle down now (.) we haven't got all day to get through this stuff (1.0) keep ties on please okay (.) yeah (.) okay and and top buttons done up James (2.0) so can we turn (.) can we turn to what we we were doing last week okay (.) ionic bonding page nine

A: page ten

T: what

A: page ten (.) it's on

B: // yeah it's on page ten

T: okay thanks page ten (.) fine okay now what do we remember (.) remember from last week about

C: // nothing

T: no not nothing (.) what about

B: // no it is nothing sir (.) we had sports day since then didn't we

T: well sports day doesn't wipe everything from (.) from your memory does it now (2.0) so what can you tell me about what happens to atoms (.) what is it that happens to atoms in ionic bonding (4.0) Melanie (1.0) what happens

A: erm (2.0) it's (.) they don't (.) they don't

T: // think about electrons

A: right yeah (.) well with electrons they like they like (.) have them when

B: // no-one remembers nothing about this

T: anything (.) remembers anything about this

B: right

A: // yeah

T: okay no (.) we do remember (.) let's just settle down and focus now right (1.0) if you don't get this it's you who has to do the exams so you really need to get this bit (2.0) in ionic bonding atoms lose or gain electrons to form (2.0) what do they form (3.0) James

B: ions (.) is it (.) ions yeah

T: yep ions (.) great okay (.) yes Tash erm (.) yes

D: sorry but erm (.) it's really hot in here sir (.) please may I (.) can I

B: // yeah

T: // okay well open the window (3.0) right so what are ions please

3. The text below is a chatroom conversation between two school friends.

What do you observe about the influence of technology on the language of this text?   *[48 marks]*

hani_ani:	hey rosie hw u doin? havnt see u for time
Bubblicious:	**i no! am cool chik hw u 2? how was tenerife?**
hani_ani:	BRILL!!!!!! the guys are soooo hot there!!
Bubblicious:	**naughty! u stil seein Billy?**
hani_ani:	lol nah, he's weird man! dmped him
Bubblicious:	**Ahhh! He wuz cool! Mite giv im a call lol!! nah fair enuff. Lookin fwd 2 going bak?**
hani_ani:	Sort of. Gonna ave 2 do sum work this yr tho
Bubblicious:	**yeh, cant wait :'-(**
hani_ani:	newayz u wanna do somethin l8tr man? Catch up a bit?
Bubblicious:	**love 2 bt no dosh :(u could cum round 2 mine?**
hani_ani:	Cud do. Wot time?
Bubblicious:	**Hw bout 8. cud watch a film or sommat....??**
hani_ani:	Cool! I'll be ther @ 8
hani_ani:	bysie byes xxxx
Bubblicious:	**XXXXXXXXX**

Spoken Language

Joy of untold joys — time to learn all about talking and stuff. Spoken language refers to the patterns and styles of language you use to communicate every time you open your mouth. Unless you're doing that hilarious goldfish impression again.

Spoken language has **Two Main Purposes**

1) **To convey meaning** — when you need to **explain something** to someone, or **give orders** or **instructions**, you use language as a means of **clarification**, so that the listener will **understand** you.

2) **To demonstrate attitudes and values** — language lets you offer **opinions** on subjects, and get your **point of view across**.

Chris promised to give conversation a chance next time.

The **Content** of spoken language **Depends** on its **Context**

Spoken language is usually the most **efficient** way for speakers to communicate with each other. As with written language, the way a spoken text is **constructed** can be affected by **external** features.

1) The **audience** or **person being addressed** — it could be someone the speaker has known for years, or thousands of people that they've never met before.

2) The **background** of the author or individual speaker — this will affect their **word choices**, **grammatical constructions**, etc.

3) The **location** and **purpose** of the text — speakers use language differently depending on where the conversation is taking place, and what's being talked about.

Spoken language can be **Formal** or **Informal**

1) **Formal** speech is used in situations when you **don't really know** the people you're talking to.

2) You might also use formal speech in a situation where you want to **show respect**, like a **job interview**.

3) It's most common in **prepared** speeches — the speaker is reading from **pre-planned, written notes**.

4) Formal spoken language is more likely to use **complex** and mainly **complete grammatical structures**.

---

1) **Informal** speech is generally used **among friends** or in situations where there's **no need** for formality or preparation.

2) It includes mostly **colloquial language**, which is casual and familiar.

3) It has **simpler** and often **incomplete grammatical structures**, more **familiar vocabulary**, more **slang** words and **dialect** features.

Speech can be **Individual** or involve **More Than One Person**

Individual speech is often known as a **monologue**. Monologues convey **internal thoughts**, **opinions** or **experiences**.

1) The term 'monologue' is usually used for a **scripted performance** (a dramatic monologue), but it can also include any **individual** speaking for a longer period of time than normal.

2) Monologues are directed at listeners who make **no spoken contribution**.

3) They can be can be **prepared** or **spontaneous**.

Dialogue is **spoken** language that involves **more than one** speaker.

1) A dialogue is a **conversation** involving two or more people — they use language to **interact** with each other.

2) Dialogue exchanges can be **short**, but in longer conversations one of the speakers may take the **major role**, with the others mainly listening and only **contributing occasionally**.

3) Dialogue can be prepared or spontaneous. Most conversations between characters on TV or in plays or films are **scripted** by a writer, but conversations between you and your friends are **unprepared** — in spontaneous dialogue speakers **respond** to the different **cues and contexts** that come up as the conversation goes on.

Spoken Language

Spoken Language Functions *in different ways*

There are **five** categories of **spoken language**, which are used in different situations.

1) **Interactional language** is the language of **informal speech**. It has a **social** function — its purpose is to **develop relationships** between speakers.

The speakers exchange personal information. →

> **A:** *so what're you studying when you get there?*
> **B:** *I'm going to be doing astronomy*
> **A:** *no way (2.0) so am I! I'll see you in lectures*

← Asking a question guarantees a response and keeps the interaction going.

2) **Referential language** provides the listener with **information**. It's used to **refer** to **objects** or to **abstract** concepts. The speaker **assumes knowledge** from the listener. The listener has to understand the **context** before they can make sense of the **references**.

> ***the parcel*** *is being delivered* **here** *at* **two o'clock**

This wouldn't make sense to the listener unless they knew that a parcel was expected.

The listener wouldn't understand this reference unless they knew where *here* was.

This assumes that the listener knows what day the parcel is expected, and whether it's more likely to be delivered at two o'clock in the morning or in the afternoon.

3) **Expressive language** highlights the speaker's **emotions**, **feelings** and **attitudes**. The language shows the speaker's judgements or feelings about another person, event or situation.

It's likely to contain adverbs to make the statements forceful

> *this* **really** *can't be allowed to continue (.) my friends (3.0) it's a* **total disgrace**

Emotive adjectives make the statements subjective

4) **Transactional language** is about **getting information** or **making a deal**, e.g. buying or selling. It has a specific purpose, so it's driven by '**needs and wants**' rather than **sociability**.

A direct request for information is followed by a direct answer. →

> **A:** *could you tell me where the soup is please?*
> **B:** *it's on aisle 7 (.) right by the croutons*

5) **Phatic language** is used for **social purposes** rather than to convey serious meaning, e.g. when someone comments about the weather as a means of **initiating a conversation**. They don't want to have a meteorological discussion with you, but it starts a conversation that (usually) quickly moves on to other subjects. Phatic communication is also called '**small talk**'.

The speaker doesn't expect these questions to be answered. →

> *did you see that rain before? it was unbelievable (2.0) I'm not too late am I?*

Practice Questions

Q1 Explain in your own words the difference between formal and informal spoken language.

Q2 What's the difference between a monologue and dialogue?

Q3 Describe the features and function of referential spoken language.

Essay Question

Q1 Describe the different types of spoken language and suggest where each might be used.

What about people that actually want a meteorological discussion with you?

Just leg it. Pure and simple. It does sort of make me wonder what weathermen or weatherwomen talk about after they've had the small talk. Maybe they talk about things they're interested in, like... I don't know... jazz, or European cinema. I don't trust them though, with their funny laser-thumbs, always changing that map on the wall behind them... making it rain a lot.

Speech Features

Who are you calling speech features? Oh... oh right. These pages will give you some all-important features of spontaneous and prepared speech. These are pretty important — more building blocks for your analysis in the exam.

Speech can be *Prepared* or *Spontaneous*

You can either know exactly what you're about to say, or you can make it up as you go along. Most people prefer the second option — spontaneous conversation comes naturally to most of us, because of these basic differences:

Prepared speech

1) Worked out **in advance**.
2) Designed for specific **audience and purpose**.
3) Needs to be **well written** (so is usually **formal** and in Standard English).
4) Is **performed** or **delivered** to try and make an impact.
5) Needs to **maintain the interest** of listeners (who may or may not be known to the speaker).
6) Examples include **political speeches** and **sermons**.

Spontaneous speech

1) **Not prepared** or written down beforehand.
2) Delivered **on the spot** as soon as, or shortly after, the idea comes to the speaker.
3) Usually **informal** (depending on context).
4) Usually shared with people **known to the speaker**.
5) Majority of spontaneous speech is **in response to** another speaker.

Ross probably should've put the vacuum appliance down before starting his speech.

Prepared and *Spontaneous* Speech are *Very Different*

If you apply **language frameworks** to prepared and spontaneous speech, you can see how different they are.

Lexis
- **Prepared speech** — the lexis is likely to be **standardised** and formal. Speakers have time to think about their word choices, so the vocabulary is more **sophisticated** and **technical**.
- **Spontaneous speech** — the lexis is likely to be **non-standard**. The informal context means **slang** and **dialect** forms are used more.

Grammar
- **Prepared speech** — the structure of sentences follows standard **grammatical rules** and pauses in the speech are controlled by **punctuation**. Speakers don't tend to use many **contractions**.
- **Spontaneous speech** — non-standard **agreements**, non-standard or **irregular tenses**, and **double negatives** are common in conversation, e.g. *I done it, We was planning to, I never told him nothing.*

Formality / Audience
- **Prepared speech** — speeches are aimed at an **audience**. The language is carefully chosen to persuade the audience in some way. Prepared speeches usually **address** the audience **directly** (the speaker uses *I* or *we*, and *you*). They're often **formal** to create a feeling of **prestige**.
- **Spontaneous speech** — most spontaneous speech is **private** and only meant for the speakers. Conversations that take place in **public places** (over a shop counter etc.) or between strangers are usually more **formal** than private ones.

Prepared and spontaneous speech also have some features in common:

1) **Discourse structure** — a prepared speech has a beginning, middle, and end. **Themes** and **ideas** are introduced at different points, and the whole thing is usually written to end on a **positive note**, so that the audience go away with a **lasting impression**. Spontaneous speech also has **formulaic** beginnings and endings (see p.64-65).

2) **Non-verbal communication** — relates to body language, gestures and facial expressions. It **emphasises** certain words or phrases in both prepared and spontaneous speech, but can also be **disruptive** if it's overdone.

3) **Prosodic and paralinguistic features** — include stress, rhythm, pitch, tempo and intonation. They're useful in prepared speech, where a speaker can use the devices to keep an audience **interested** over a long period of time.

Speech Features

Spontaneous speech has many Unique Features

Even though **spontaneous speech** shares some features with prepared spoken English, it has lots of **specific features**. Look at the following **conversation** between two people:

> Ellipsis is where part of a grammatical structure is omitted without affecting understanding, e.g. *(Are) You going to come round later?* It makes the tone more casual than the full version.

> Phatic expressions play a key role in spontaneous speech, especially when you're initiating a conversation. The comments have no great meaning or interest in themselves, but are designed to help conversations get started.

> False starts regularly occur in conversation. The speaker changes their train of thought halfway through, and begins the utterance again.

> Back-channelling is used to feed back to a speaker that what they're saying is being understood, e.g. *I see* or another repeated utterance. You can also give feedback non-verbally e.g. nodding or shaking your head.

Speaker 1:	alright mate
Speaker 2:	hi Dan (.) how's it going
Speaker 1:	yeah not bad thanks how are you
Speaker 2:	good thanks (.) enjoying the sun
Speaker 1:	makes nice change dunt it (1) I mean
Speaker 2:	// yeah (2) you get my message the other day
Speaker 1:	um, yeah, I think so (.) about (1) er (.) you're having a party
Speaker 2:	// party yeah
Speaker 1:	// oh yeah
Speaker 2:	yeah on sat (.) er tomorrow night
Speaker 1:	// oh yeah
Speaker 2:	down at mine (.) d'ya know where that is
Speaker 1:	// yeah // yeah no um I know it
Speaker 2:	cool (.) gonna come down then
Speaker 1:	coursa will mate (.) sounds good
Speaker 2:	nice one (3) er, see you there then
Speaker 1:	yep, probably see you later

> Deictic expressions are pointers that refer the listener backwards, forwards or outside a text. Most common are words such as *this*, *that*, *here*, and *there*. You can't understand deictic expressions unless you know their context.

> Hedging shows uncertainty in a conversation — words like *perhaps* or *maybe* are used to weaken the force of what you're saying.

> Elision is the slurring together of sounds or syllables, e.g. *gonna* rather than *going to* — this saves time, and is less formal.

> Non-fluency features are devices that interrupt the flow of talk. Hesitation or repetition, fillers such as *er* or *um*, interruptions and overlaps are all non-fluency features.

Practice Questions

Q1   Give a key difference in the use of grammar in prepared speech as opposed to spontaneous speech.

Q2   How can paralinguistic and prosodic features help speakers?

Q3   Give three examples of phatic expressions.

Essay Question

Q1   Discuss the differences between prepared and spontaneous speech, with reference to lexis, grammar and formality.

Everyone uses phatic expressions — even if they're not that phat...

Hopefully, you'll recognise some of these features from conversations you've had in the past with people you know (and probably people you don't). If you don't, good work. You're obviously the finest conversationalist since Talky McChatterlot, who never hedged, or false-started, or used phatic expressions or anything. He was dead dull though.

Conversation and Turn-taking

If you've ever had a conversation, you'll know that you can't just rabbit on all the way through... unless it's a conversation with yourself... in which case, sorry for interrupting. But if there are two people involved — learn the rules.

Some features occur in All Conversations

No matter who you find yourself talking to, the devices for **starting** and **ending** conversations are usually the same.

1) **Openings** — an informal conversation may begin with a simple **familiar starter**. These are usually **greetings**, such as *hello*, or *alright?* More formal conversations often include **inquiries** like *I wonder if you could help me?* to get someone's **attention**.

> Speaker 1: *good morning*
> Speaker 2: *hello (.) can I help you?*

2) **Responses** — familiar openings (see above) invite a particular response.

> S1: *hello (.) can I help you?*
> S2: *I'm just browsing thanks.*

3) **Adjacency pairs** — **short**, **familiar exchanges** of conversation that follow **predictable** patterns.

> S1: *how are you?*
> S2: *I'm fine thanks*

4) **Signalling closure** — speech indicators and other non-verbal signs can be used to show that a conversation is **drawing to a close**.

> S1: *he fell down a manhole once.*
> S2: *really? well (.) time I was off.*

Some features depend on the Individual Speakers

Switching and turn-taking

1) The person speaking at any given time may be aware that **someone else** wants to speak.
2) In an orderly conversation they **invite** the switch to another speaker e.g. by **pausing**, or trying to make an **emphatic** final statement.
3) **Domineering** speakers sometimes choose to **ignore** this, meaning other speakers have to break into the conversation by **interrupting**, or just **stay silent**.

> S1: *I can't believe he didn't see it*
> S2: *why not (1) it wasn't a penalty (2) what do you think?*
> S3: *I think it probably was*
> S2: *that's why you're not a referee*
> S1: *it's pretty hard to work out*
> S2:   *// maybe if you weren't watching*

Tag questions

1) These are attached to the **end of statements**, and **invite responses** from other speakers.
2) They're used by speakers who are seeking some **feedback**.
3) This could be because they're feeling **uncomfortable**, or because they're trying to **control** the conversation by bringing other people into it.

> S1: *this is an issue that we need to resolve quickly <u>isn't it</u>?*

Topic Shifts

1) **Topic shifts** are when speakers **change** the **subject** of the conversation.
2) They move the conversation forward or **change** its **focus**.
3) They're usually started by the domineering speaker trying to control the **content** and **direction** of a conversation.

> S1: *so I said carbonara*
> S2: *right (2) did you ever hear back from Dave?*

Feedback

1) When someone's speaking, people give **verbal** and **non-verbal** signs that they're **listening** to them
2) For example, brief comments, nodding or shaking your head, smiling, frowning, etc.

> S1: *no-one told me it was a sponge*
> S2: *mm-hmm*

Conversation and Turn-taking

Different *Techniques* are involved at different *Stages* of a *Conversation*

Getting involved / Initiating conversation

1) Most participants in a conversation will offer a contribution **without waiting** to be asked — if you waited to be asked to speak in every conversation, you might **never** speak at all.

2) You might get a conversation started by showing an **interest** in the other people involved.

3) If you're talking to an **unfamiliar person**, appropriate **phatic expressions** and **questioning** can help get things started, e.g. you can use **tag questions** to initiate **responses**.

Sustaining conversation

1) Fluent speaking (following **adjacency patterns** and **turn-taking rules**), showing an interest (**feedback**) and generally enjoying talking are all factors that help people **sustain** conversation.

2) **Speaker empathy** is important — if people are exploring **shared interests** or **opinions** then the conversation is more likely to be sustained. Listeners might make it clear that they share the speaker's views by using feedback, e.g. *mm* and *yeah*.

Ending conversation

1) **Social convention** makes us not want to appear rude, cut people short or walk away when they're not ready — so **phatic expressions** are used to **signal closure** in a socially recognisable way, e.g. *I should probably get going*.

2) There are also **non-verbal** cues that signal a speaker is about to end the conversation e.g. starting to **get up** from a seat, or increasing the **distance** between the speakers.

The conversation got heated as they tried to work out who'd thought of the fancy dress costume first.

Participants *Manage* and *Control* conversations

In an orderly conversation, you take **turns** speaking with other people. However, not all conversations are orderly and it's rare to find one where each speaker actually waits their turn — it depends on the **individuals** involved.

Prepared / Formal situations

1) These are the types of conversation where there is a defined power relationship between the participants, e.g. conducting an **interview** with someone or being interviewed yourself.

2) **Prepared situations** (like a tutorial, job interview or debate) have a **specific subject** or subject area on the agenda. You may not know precisely how the conversation will go, but you know what is **likely** to be discussed, and the level of **formality** you're expected to use.

3) There's usually a person **overtly** in charge of the exchanges, like a lecturer, interviewer or chairperson, whose **authority** to change the conversation at will is **already acknowledged** before it starts.

Unprepared / Informal situations

1) **Informal** social conversations are less likely to be prepared, and could involve any topic, but these still tend to be **controlled** by certain individuals.

2) People who are **louder**, **quicker** and more **forceful** than other speakers often **dominate informal conversations**.

3) It is easy for less confident and less assertive speakers to be **inhibited** or **intimidated**, and to end up contributing very little (for more on conversations and power, see p.50-53).

Practice Questions

Q1   Give an example of a tag question, and describe its purpose.

Q2   What are adjacency pairs, and how are they used in conversation?

Essay Question

Q1   Discuss the techniques speakers use to initiate, manage, control, sustain and end conversations.

You say potato, I say pipe down for ONE MINUTE so I can get a word in...

Is that too much to ask? Right then. You should now have all the tools you need for analysing spoken language, whether it's prepared speeches (when you need to think mainly about purpose and effect), or spontaneous conversation (where you need to think about features of interaction). And for once, eavesdropping would be really good practice.

Sources and Exam Questions

You'll find plenty of spoken language in the first section of the AQA B exam paper. We've put this question in to help you pick out the important features from different types of spoken language texts, but it's not quite the same as the question you'll get in section A of your exam (see Section 7).

---

1) Study the three texts below, **A**, **B** and **C**.

Analyse and compare the use of language by the speakers in these texts.

In your answer you should consider:

- the features of spontaneous speech
- the uses of standard and non-standard grammar
- how the texts are controlled and managed.

Text A — Conversation between a customer and a newsagent.

A: now then Sam

B: now then (.) been sent to get the paper

A: yes here we are (.) bit late delivering today

B: oh yeah

A: yeah it's a right pain (1.0) here I saw your lad the other day (.) he back now from

B: // mm   // aye yeah (.) yeah back from university

A: comes round quick doesn't it

B: quick yeah (.) yeah he's back three months now

A: // three months

B: // aye (.) I er I wanted to ask actually (1.0) he's gonna need some er some work you see (.) while he's (.) but he doesn't drive so I mean you don't know anyone in the village who might need (.) need a bit of work done do you

A: oh aye yeah (.) I see (.) long time to go with no work is three months (2.0) I'll have a think

B: // mm I mean I think he's willing for most things (.) odd jobs and

A: // odd jobs like (.) mm (2.0) tell you what (.) some of the older people might need a hand in their gardens (.) you know mowing the lawn and that

B: // yeah that'll be

A: tell you what (.) write his name and a contact number on a card (.) I can put it up there with the others on the board over there

B: oh cheers yeah (.) oh that'll be great yeah thanks (1.0) if you hear anyone mentioning needing help in the meantime give us a nod will you

A: no problem mate

Text B — Extract from a job interview.

X: (*the interviewer*) you must be Matthew (2.0) come in and have a seat

Y: (*the candidate*) yep that's ri- (2.0) oh right (.) thanks

X: you found the office alright then did you?

Y: er (.) yep it was fine (.) I had a map so

X: // good good (.) we'll get started then (1.0) I don't want to keep you too long (.) basically what's going to happen is I'll ask you a few questions about your suitability for the role (1.0) and then we'll have a little chat about the company so you can see if you like us (.) and we can see if we like you (2.0) that sound ok?

Y: yeah grea- (1.0) um (.) yeah that sounds fine

X: excellent (.) so (2.0) I see from your CV and application that you've worked in radio before?

Y: Yep (1.0) yes I

Sources and Exam Questions

(Text B contd.)

X: // why don't you tell me a little bit about that

Y: OK (3.0) well basically (.) um (.) it was a hospital radio station and (1.0) er I had to go round wards and get requests from people that were going to listen to the show (.) and (2.0) um (.) sort of put it together you know

X: mmm-hmm (1.0) right OK (1.0) and did you get a chance to do any work behind the desks?

Y: Yeah (.) yeah I did (.) er (2.0) at first I was only really allowed to speak on air (1.0) you know, probably a good thing (2.0) but then I started to learn a bit about the presenting and I got

X: // and then you got a shot at DJ-ing?

Y: er (.) yeah (1.0) they let me loose after that

X: good (.) great (1.0) so did you enjoy that or did you prefer producing the shows you were working on?

Text C — Speech by a company director to the company's employees.

ladies and gentlemen (1.0) err ladies and gentlemen (2.0) can (.) can you hear me OK at the back there?

(*indistinct responses*)

err (.) ladies and gentlemen thank you all very (.) very much for coming today (2.0) I (.) I know some of you were only given very short notice of this meeting (.) and I apologise for that but thanks for making the effort to be here (2.0) I wish I had better news to share with you (1.0) but as some of you will already know (1.0) I'm afraid I don't

it's difficult to know how best to put this (2.0) but here goes (.)

many of you will already be aware that the company has been struggling of late to break even (1.0) what with the increasing costs of production (.) the high cost of borrowing (1.0) and so on (2.0) and so (.) management has been forced into the kind of decision that we hoped that we were never going to have to make

(*murmuring from the floor*)

the branch is going to have to close down in order to keep alive the chances of us keeping going elsewhere (5.0) we aim to find work elsewhere for as many of you as possible (.) especially our younger workers (1.0) but we simply can't provide enough for everyone (1.0) so with the greatest regret (1.0) and I assure it is with the greatest regret and we're not smiling behind your backs (2.0) we are going to have to offer redundancy packages to some of you (.)

I want you all to be aware that a redundancy package in no way suggests that we think that you are no longer valued by us (1.0) but we simply can't avoid doing this if we're to have any chance of continuing to hold our place in the market in the future (3.0) we have to be pragmatic about this — we have no choice (3.0)

Les (.) the branch manager (.) will be speaking to each of you individually within the next few days (1.0) I don't envy him this for one moment (1.0) so that you're all in the picture as quickly as possible.

I can't really say very much more (2.0) other than to emphasise once again how much it hurts me to have to stand up and do this (2.0) thank you all very (.) very much

Transcription Key

(.) *Micropause*

(2.0) *Pause in seconds*

// *Interruption / overlapping speech*

Purpose

All the texts you'll see will have been written for a purpose, otherwise there wouldn't have been any point in writing them in the first place. To identify the main reason a text was written you need to analyse the language it uses.

Texts usually have one of Four Main Purposes

1) Written texts usually try to achieve one of the following purposes.

> 1. **Inform** e.g. newspaper   2. **Instruct** e.g. cookbook   3. **Persuade** e.g. advert   4. **Entertain** e.g. comic

Not all texts slot neatly into these categories, e.g. a film review might be informative, entertaining and persuasive.

2) Despite this, you can usually work out the primary function of a text by looking at its language and presentation. To find out the **purpose** of a text you need to apply these **frameworks**:

> - **Lexis** — vocabulary / specific words
> - **Graphology** — how the text is arranged
> - **Grammar** — sentence length and structure
> - **Semantics** — meaning (actual or hidden)

Informative Texts are Factual

There are many different types of informative text. Informative writing needs to contain **knowledge** or **facts** that readers want to know, like the latest news in a newspaper.

1) Informative texts are **structured clearly** so they're easy to **understand**.
   They might include presentational features such as headings / subheadings, bullet points, boxes and illustrations.

2) The information is presented in a way that's **suitable** for the **intended audience**. If it's intended for children, the language is **simple** and **less detailed**. An informative text for an older audience might use more **complex** language — assuming that the reader has some **previous knowledge**.

3) The text may include **specialist** or **technical terms**, and explain them.

4) The tone is usually **serious**. Informative texts don't generally include **opinions** or **comments**.
   Some informative texts simply consist of times and dates, e.g. a train timetable.

5) Informative texts are usually written in the **third person**, using *he*, *she*, or *it*.

Instructional Texts tell you How to do something

These texts are similar to informative texts because they include **information**. However, the main function of an instructional text is to show the reader **how** to do something **practical**. They have a **clear**, **structured** style:

1) Instructional texts usually include **chronological**, **numbered** sections.

2) They use graphological devices such as **bullet points** and **headings**.

3) The instructions are often given as **imperative** sentences e.g. *Add the butter, sugar and flour to the mixture.*

4) The text may use **second person** forms (e.g. *you do this*) to address the reader directly.

5) The lexis is **straightforward** and **uncomplicated**, but can be **subject-specific** (e.g. *beat, whisk, fold* in cooking).

Persuasive Texts aim to Change Your Mind

Persuasive texts try to either **influence** the reader's opinions or **persuade** them to do something.

1) They often use **first person address** (*I* and *we*) to communicate the speaker's **feelings** and include the listeners. Possessive pronouns like *our* and *your* also **personally** involve the reader in the views expressed in the text.

2) They often use **emotive adjectives** and **subjective judgements** to provoke emotional and intellectual responses.

3) They use facts, statistics and other **evidence** to support the main argument, linked together with connectives such as *therefore, because,* and *however* to create a **logical route** to a conclusion.

4) They might use eye-catching **graphology** (p.28-29), such as **logos**, **capitalization** and **colour**, to attract the reader's attention and **stress** the importance of a particular point or argument.

Purpose

There are many Different Types of Entertainment texts

1) **Entertainment texts** include novels, stories, articles, verses, songs, poetry, plays, biographies and autobiographies.

2) Even though there's a big **range** of entertainment texts, they tend to have **several features in common**:

> - **Sophisticated** language
> - **Figurative** language
> - **Extensive** vocabulary
> - Often **complex structure**
> - Varied **sentence types**
> - Eye-catching **layout**

3) These techniques help the writers of entertainment texts to express personal **feelings** and produce **poetic** thoughts and ideas.

4) Writers also use these features to influence how the audience **experiences** the text. Entertainment texts can help audiences **escape** from reality, **frighten** and **shock** them, affect them **emotionally** or make them **think**.

5) Some writers might choose to **change** or **ignore** these **expected conventions** to achieve **different effects**.

Texts that Analyse Language are called Commentaries

A **commentary** or **language analysis** (which you'll be asked to produce in your exam) needs to focus on the following areas:

1) The **linguistic choices** made by the writer.
2) **Distinctive features** of the style or genre chosen by the writer.
3) The influence of the **context** upon the language choices.
4) What **effects** were **intended** or **achieved** in the text.

Linguistic terminology is all very well, but sometimes the only appropriate medium is contemporary dance.

As a writer, commentaries enable you to do the following things:

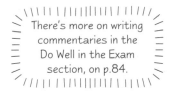

There's more on writing commentaries in the Do Well in the Exam section, on p.84.

1) Communicate your **knowledge** and **understanding** of how language works by applying it to a particular piece of writing or speech.
2) Use appropriate **linguistic terminology** to explain your points.
3) Demonstrate your knowledge of appropriate **frameworks of language**.

Practice Questions

Q1 How can you tell if the purpose of a text is to inform?

Q2 Which type of text (informative, instructive, persuasive or entertaining) is more likely to use sophisticated language and a variety of sentence structures?

Q3 In persuasive texts, why is the reader often directly addressed in the second person *you*?

Essay Questions

Q1 What sort of language would writers use to make their purpose obvious to an audience in the following types of text: reference book, feature article for a magazine and an advertisement for a charity.

Revision guide texts aim to make you really really really smart...

And that's just the start. I also aim to solve the world's climate problems, but I've yet to work out how to do it using only a handful of verbs and some prepositions. I imagine the eventual solution will be glorious and I'll be hailed as a genius. For now, I'll just advise you to try and be a better student by learning everything there is to know about purpose.

Audience

It stands to reason that if texts are written for a particular purpose, they're probably going to be written for a particular audience too. You should be able to identify a text's target audience by analysing the type of language it uses.

The **Audience** is the group of people that the **Text** is **Aimed At**

Intended audiences can vary from the very **general** (e.g. 'adults'), to the very **specific** (e.g. 'females over 30 with young children').

1) Writers **tailor** their texts for different audiences and purposes.

2) To work out the audience of a text, you need to be able to **recognise** and **describe** how a text **suits** a particular kind of reader.

3) You can find **clues** about the audience, their age and relative status, and how the writer **feels about them** in the language of a text, e.g. if a text contains simple sentences and basic lexis, it's likely to be for a young audience.

A writer may or may not **Know Their Audience**

A lot depends on **how familiar** the writer or speaker is with their audience:

Known audience

1) The writer might use **personal pronouns** like *I* and *you*. This writing is most often found in memos, personal letters, diaries and stories.

2) The writer may use language that expresses **emotion**, **feelings** or **opinions**.

3) A writer might also have a **target audience** they know quite a lot about e.g. science fiction fans, or film buffs, or supporters of a particular political party. The writer will choose language that they **expect** will be understood and have an effect on members of the target audience.

Unknown audience

Sometimes the text is for an audience that is **unfamiliar**. This type of writing is often found in **academic** or **instructive texts**. The main characteristics are:

1) The writer doesn't **acknowledge** the reader directly as it's usually written in the third person.

2) There is no expression of **personal feeling** and no use of first or second person **pronouns** (*I* or *you*).

3) The text is quite **formal** — it may use formal vocabulary, imperative sentences (in instructive texts) or the **passive voice**. Texts for unknown audiences deal with **serious** subject matter rather than entertainment.

You can **Work Out** the **Intended Audience** of a text

To **identify** the intended **audience** of a text, you need to look at the **style** of the text, its **content**, the choice of **vocabulary** and the **tone**.

1) **Style** — **formal** and **serious** writing is usually for an **older audience**. If the text is **informal** and more **light-hearted** it's often aimed at a **younger audience**. To narrow down the audience further, you need to look at the content of the text.

2) **Content** — the text might be about a **general topic** like global warming, or it might be something **very specific** like the writer's new trainers. The first would have a very **broad** audience, but the second would be aimed at a much smaller audience.

3) **Lexis** — if there are any **complex**, **specialist** or **technical** words, the audience are probably experts — they will already be **familiar** with the jargon. If there are no specialist words, and the lexis is **uncomplicated** and easy to follow, this suggests a **younger** or **less specialist** audience.

4) **Tone** — the tone reflects the purpose of a text, e.g. an informative text would have a serious tone. The tone can also say something about the audience, e.g. a **serious** tone suggests a **mature** or **interested** audience.

5) **Formality** — formal texts (e.g. reports, articles) are usually aimed at **older**, **professional** audiences (with the exception of textbooks, which are aimed at students). Other texts, e.g. e-mails, are more **informal** and **friendly** as the audience is a **known person** or **group**.

Audience

Texts need to **Suit** their **Readership**

Texts are more **accessible** if they are tailored to suit their audience.

1) The text needs to be **tailored** depending on whether it's aimed at children or adults, e.g. different language is used on a **newspaper front page** compared to a **children's comic**.

2) Texts can sometimes be **gender-specific**, aimed at male or female audiences, e.g. the style and content of *Cosmopolitan* is different to that of *FHM*.

3) The **expertise** of the audience is also an important factor — if the audience are experts then the lexis can be more **specialised** than if the text is for a general readership.

Texts can have **Multiple Audiences**

1) Texts may have **more** than one audience, each of which may respond **differently** to it.

2) For example, a children's story is principally aimed at a **young audience**. However it is an **adult** who will decide whether to buy the book — so it needs to **appeal** to the adult as well.

3) If you've ever seen the film **Shrek**® (2001), you'll have seen how a text can appeal to **lots of different** audiences. It's designed to work on **different levels**, with plenty for kids but also jokes that only adults will understand.

Audiences of **Spoken Discourse** vary too

1) The **content** of a spoken discourse can **reveal** the audience, e.g. the **content** of a **university lecture** reveals that it's intended for students specialising in a subject.

2) The talk could be **formal**, like a public speech, or **colloquial**, like a conversation. The level of formality shows the **relationship** of the listener to the speaker, e.g. you speak **respectfully** and **politely** to someone in a position of **authority**, but **casually** with friends.

3) In the same way, **long complex** sentences would be appropriate in an academic lecture or formal context. **Shorter sentences** and the use of **contractions** (like *won't* or *can't*) as well as **interruptions** and **non-fluency** features are more frequently found in informal conversations.

4) Use of a **regional dialect**, or words and grammatical constructions not considered to be **'correct'** English, can help place a target audience **geographically**, **socially** or **ethnically**.

"We've been talking for 3 days now — I should probably get back to work."

Practice Questions

Q1 What are the main differences between a text that is written for a known audience and a text that is written for an unknown audience?

Q2 Name at least two elements of a text that you need to analyse in order to work out the intended audience.

Q3 Explain how analysing the lexis of a text can help you understand the audience.

Essay Question

Q1 What differences would you expect to see between an instruction text for children and an instruction text for adults? Explain your answer with reference to style, content, lexis, tone and formality.

If you're aiming for a target audience, make sure you don't miss...

For some reason people get really uppity about texts pinging around and hitting them in the chops when they're not expecting it. But on a serious note, don't forget that writers identify audiences through the attitudes, beliefs and needs they think a group might have or want. Then they can tailor texts specifically to attract the audience (more on this later).

Genre

Boy, do those linguists love sorting things into groups. CDs, clothes, pens — you name it, they'll sort it. But the thing they love to sort more than anything else is texts. Genre is one way of classifying and organising texts into different categories.

Genre groups texts that have Similar Features

Similar types of texts often seem to follow a **distinctive pattern**. A group of texts with the same features is called a **genre**.

1) **Genre conventions** make **written** and **spoken** communication more **efficient**.

2) When you read a text from a particular **genre**, you have certain **expectations** about it.

3) Knowing **what kind of text** you're reading lets you **predict** what form it will take.

Knowing about genres means you can **classify** language. It allows a reader to form **expectations** about the text based on their **experience** of the **genre**.

There are Many Different Genres of Written Text

Examples of **written genres** include: letters, reports, poems, stories, advertisements, postcards, recipes, e-mails, cartoons, text-messages etc. Each genre has a different **writing style** associated with it. For example:

Letters
Formal convention:
1) Sender's address at the top
2) Date and *Dear Sir/Madam*
3) Concludes *Yours sincerely/faithfully*
4) Followed by a signature

Postcards
Abbreviated format:
1) Very informal
2) Contractions common (e.g. *won't, can't*)
3) Dashes and exclamation marks

Recipes
Step-by-step instructions:
1) Start with list of ingredients
2) Followed by numbered instructions
3) Short instructive sentences
4) May include some technical words (like *braise, simmer* or *baste*)

Text messages
Extremely informal:
1) Highly contracted language (*lol* or *btw*)
2) Emoticons (e.g. :-))
3) Language based on sound (e.g. *gr8* or *neway*)

Spoken Texts also follow Conventions

Spoken text also has its own genres with **distinctive patterns**. Spoken language is broken down into two main areas — **monologue or dialogue** (see p.60). Each spoken genre has different **conventions** associated with it. Some examples are:

Genre	Conventions
Answer-phone message	The message often begins with *"Sorry, I'm not around at the moment"* (or something similar), and is likely to end with *"Please leave a message after the beep"*.
Interview	An interviewer will often ask typical questions such as *"Why are you interested in this company / college?"*, or *"What are your strengths and weaknesses?"*.
Lesson	A lesson might begin with some questions to recap a topic, and may end with the teacher giving out homework to the class.
Radio show	A radio presenter would normally begin a show with *"Hello, and welcome to..."* and then give the name of the show and their own name. They'd typically refer to the listener directly as *you*, and refer to the audience and themselves collectively as *we*.

Genre

You can also Group Genres

1) As well as classifying texts into genres, you can group **similar genres** together according to how they use **language**.

2) Each group of genres is called a **field**, e.g. music, literature and conversation.

3) Each field has **field-specific lexis**, or vocabulary, that is used within that particular topic, for example:

Music
Genres — jazz, rock, classical, folk
Field-specific lexis — *CD, album, single, artist, band.*

Literature
Genres — plays, poetry, short stories, novels
Field-specific lexis — *metaphor, stanza, chapter, stage directions*

TV
Genres — game shows, soap operas, dramas, sitcoms
Field-specific lexis — *studio, script, lighting, boom, presenter*

Henry and Jonny couldn't believe they were the only ones in their field.

Genres can be Broken Down into Sub-genres

As if that's not enough, you can divide genres into smaller groups of texts, called **sub-genres**:

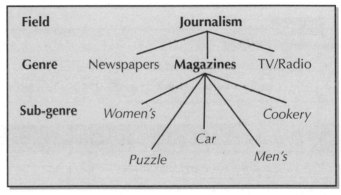

Each of these sub-genres has developed its own **specific lexis** that relates to that sub-genre in particular. For example, the word *autocue* is specific to the **sub-genre** of **TV presenting**, and *blog* relates to the **sub-genre** of **online publishing**.

Practice Questions

Q1 Why are texts categorised into different genres?

Q2 Give three examples of spoken genres.

Q3 What is a field? Give an example and list some of its field-specific lexis.

Essay Question

Q1 Choose three examples of written genres. Explain the differences between them, focusing in particular on graphology and lexis.

That's where my answerphone message has been going wrong then...

I've been using Hello, by Lionel Richie. Which I suppose is pretty unconventional, and might be the reason no one leaves me any messages. Or maybe they're not actually looking for me. Make sure you've got your head around the field / genre / sub-genre distinctions here, and learn some written and spoken examples. Then make like a new leaf and turn over.

Literary Texts

Literary texts are mainly written to entertain — people read or listen to them for pleasure. To keep the audience interested, literary texts usually contain imaginative uses of language, like experimentation with vocabulary and grammar.

Authors of Literary Texts can be very Creative

Literary texts are part of the very broad entertainment field. People read literary texts because they can:

1) **Entertain** or **amuse** the reader.
2) Affect the reader's **emotions**, e.g. make them scared, excited or sympathetic.
3) Describe the **atmosphere** of a place or setting.
4) Examine the **personality** of a **character**.
5) Influence how the reader **looks at the world**.

His wife's shopping list evoked an atmosphere mild panic.

There are Three Main Types of literary texts

The most common types of literary texts are prose (like books), poetry (like poems), and plays (er... like plays).

PROSE

- For example, novels, short stories, biography, autobiography.
- It's structured as **running text**, and divided into paragraphs and chapters (for novels).
- There are often no subsections, charts, or lists, and **usually no illustrations**.
- It has a **beginning** and usually a **definite ending**.
- The narrative is told from a certain **point of view**.

POETRY

- Poems **vary** in content, structure, style and intention.
- Some present **narrative stories**, some are written to be **performed**, others explore **emotional issues**.
- Poems are organised into **stanzas** (verses) of varying sizes.
- **Line length** can vary considerably and the poem may or may not **rhyme**.
- There are some **traditional forms** poems can take, e.g. sonnet or villanelle.
- There are also traditional **metres** (rhythms) e.g. pentameters.

PLAYS

- Plays consist of **dialogue** between characters, or (if it's a monologue) a character talking **directly** to the audience.
- They also include **stage directions** to instruct the actors and describe actions etc.
- The speech is very important, as it's the main way for the audience to **understand** the **action** and the **characters**.

All literary texts use a Narrative Voice

Writers use different **narrative voices** within literary texts.

1) A **first-person narrator** in a text tells the reader directly about their **feelings and experiences**. The text is viewed through the character's eyes.

> The moment I woke up that morning I just knew that something wasn't right. I was utterly exhausted and Ryan wouldn't stop talking...

2) A **third-person narrator** tells the story from a detached viewpoint, as a voice in their own right.

> Kit explained it to her as gently as he could; there was no point upsetting her even more. But still, poor Sarah was devastated. As soon as she got home she flung herself on the bed and was overcome with sorrow...

3) A **third-person omniscient narrator** lets the reader see into the **minds** and **thoughts** of **all** the characters.

Literary texts use lots of Figurative Language

Figurative language adds layers of meaning to texts. There's loads more on this on p.20.

1) **Imagery** creates a scene in the reader's mind e.g. *the sea was wild and stormy*.
2) A **simile** is when something is described in **comparison** to something else, e.g. *The sea is like a savage beast*.
3) A **metaphor** creates a **comparison**, like a simile, but it implies the subject and the thing it's being compared to are the **same** e.g. *the sea is a savage beast*, rather than comparing them.
4) **Personification** is a kind of metaphor, in which the **attributes** of a person are given to abstract or non-human things, for example *the sea shrieked and roared*.
5) **Symbolism** is where a word or phrase **represents something else**, e.g. the colour *red* could represent danger.

Literary Texts

Rhetorical Language is used to provide Extra Effects or Meanings

There are **two categories** of rhetorical language.

Phonological — manipulates sound. Words or phrases might be used because they sound good.

1) **Rhyme** is particularly effective in poetry because it can contribute to the **musical quality** of a verse. It unifies the poem and can **add emphasis** to certain words. There are different kinds of rhyme, including **half rhyme** — where the vowel or consonant may vary (e.g. *roll* and *tell*) and **internal rhyme** — where rhymes occur within a line itself (e.g. *in mist or cloud, on mast or shroud*).

2) **Alliteration** is the repetition of the **same consonant sound**, usually at the beginning of each word, over **two or more words together**, e.g. *sink slowly into a soothing sleep.*

3) **Assonance** is a similar repetition, but of **vowels** in the middle of words e.g. *a hoover manoeuvre.*

4) **Onomatopoeia** refers to words that sound like the noise they describe, e.g. *buzz, pop, bang.*

Structural — affects the overall meaning of a text by manipulating its structural features.

1) **Repetition** is often used to add **emphasis or persuasiveness** to a text. It can add **power** to a subject, or help a text lead to a **dramatic climax**.

2) **Parallelism** repeats **structural features**, like the construction of a **phrase**, e.g. *She jumped from the bed, and raced to the window,* which repeatedly uses the **past tense** form of the verb with the preposition and noun. An example of **non-parallelism** is something like *He loves films and to eat* — the construction of the phrases *loves film* and *to eat* are different and seem awkward to the reader.

3) **Antithesis** is when contrasting ideas or words are balanced against each other, e.g. *when there is need of silence, you speak, and when there is need of speech, you are silent.*

Dialogue can also be Very Effective

Dialogue is an especially effective device in **plays**.

1) Different characters may speak in **different ways** to influence the audience's opinions of them.

2) Dialogue helps to show the **relationships** between characters — whether they get on, or if there's **tension** between them. It also tells you about a character's **personality** through their **interactions** with other characters, e.g. if they're assertive, nervous, thoughtful, domineering, etc.

3) There are differences between dialogue in **literary texts** and **natural conversation**. In plays and novels, the dialogue tends to be **organised** and **fluent**, e.g. there is strict **turn-taking** and not much **interruption** or **hesitation**. In real-life conversation there are a lot **non-fluency features** because the dialogue is **spontaneous**.

4) **Dramatic writing** relies on **dialogue** to create and develop **characters**. This means that the atmosphere is **often implied**. In **fictional texts**, the writer can **experiment** with **language** to describe these features.

Practice Questions

Q1   What are the main purposes of literary texts?

Q2   Why might a writer choose to use a third-person narrator instead of a first-person narrator?

Q3   What is the importance of rhyme in poetry?

Essay Question

Q1   Read the opening page of a novel that you already know. How does the author use language to convey the setting, characterisation and atmosphere effectively? You should consider:

1) the ways in which the writer's attitudes and values are conveyed to the reader.

2) features of the language such as figurative and rhetorical devices, and dialogue.

Even the simplest texts are still just one thing after anauthor...

Well it's not like there's a good pun for "symbolism", is it? These pages are all about ways of manipulating language, and the effect this has on the audience of a literary text. They've got some great terms to have at your disposal in the exam — being able to pick out these sorts of features and describe their purposes in different texts will get you tonnes of marks.

Ideology and Representation

This basically covers what people think about different texts. Both writers and readers approach texts with their own attitudes. These attitudes affect what the writers write, and how the readers interpret it.

Writers show their Attitudes in their Texts

An ideology is a set of beliefs and ideas.

You can often get a sense of a writer's **opinions** and **ideology** through **how** they write and the **topics** they choose.

1) The **values** and **morals** in a text will probably depend on those held by the writer or speaker, e.g. a politician might speak about their attitude to marriage, based on the views of their particular political party or religion. This is often the case in **fictional** texts too, but not always.

2) Texts can show **prejudice** and **bias**, e.g. a writer might portray British characters sympathetically, and make their foreign characters all appear rather shady. This is an **implicit** meaning — it's not immediately obvious.

3) A writer might also show their **attitudes** quite **explicitly**, e.g. a journalist writing for a liberal newspaper might express their dislike for conservative politics.

4) Writers sometimes draw on **personal experience**, because it's easier to write about what you know, e.g. because he's been through the experience himself, a writer might describe a young gay man struggling to come out to his parents.

5) Writers' attitudes are also influenced by the social or political **environment** they're in. This is often evident in the **representation** of their **characters**, **narrator**, and the **themes** and **issues** that the text tries to deal with.

Social and historical context
- Texts often **reflect** the **concerns** of a **society** at a particular **time**.
- For example — the James Bond books often feature Soviet villains being thwarted by Bond, a British spy. They were written during the **Cold War** period of the 1950s and 60s, so they reflect the fear that countries like Britain and America had of the communist USSR.
- A text is a **product** of the **culture** and **time** it's written or set in — you wouldn't expect a spy novel written in the UK today to feature Russian Communist villains.

Writers can show their Attitudes through their Characters

1) Writers might draw on **stereotypes** when they're **constructing characters**, e.g. they might present a character who is an MP as a middle-aged man with grey hair who wears a suit.

2) A writer may create characters based on how the **media** represents groups of people (see p.54-55). This includes **stereotypes** like portraying a group of young people as a *gang of hoodies*.

3) The writer might **unconsciously** reflect the views or values of **wider society**. Someone from a Western culture, writing nowadays, might refer to a character as '*lovely and slim*'. This would reflect the **broader** attitude in Western society that being slim is beautiful.

4) You can also get an idea of a writer's values and beliefs from how they **subvert stereotypes**, e.g. a feminist author might write about workplaces and homes dominated by women.

A writer's Language Choices can Influence the Reader

The language of a text is often **manipulated** to create certain emotions or reactions in the reader. The **manipulation** of the reader is a frequent tool that writers use to **increase** the **impact** of their texts or even to **subvert conventions**.

1) Politicians delivering speeches about social problems want listeners to feel like they **share** their desire to solve the problem. They use **inclusive pronouns** like *we* and *us* to position the listener as a **confidant** and therefore a potential **supporter**.

2) A charity leaflet might use emotive words like *cruelty* to **represent** the **treatment** of people or groups, or *desperate* to convey the **seriousness** of their situation.

3) Writers can use **different viewpoints** in novels and articles. First person narrators can bring readers **close** to the text and they can get **emotionally involved**. Third person omniscient narratives give **insights** into characters and allow the reader to step back and be **objective**.

4) Writers can also **subvert** these conventions to manipulate the reader, e.g. using a first person narrator who turns out to be **completely unreliable**.

Ideology and Representation

Writers still have to Appeal to Readers

Writers know that audiences **approach** texts in different ways so they have to represent ideas and characters that readers can identify with.

1) Members of an audience bring their own **experience**, personality, background, prejudices, beliefs and values to their interpretation of any text. These factors shape how a reader **views** a situation or **feels** about a character.

2) Writers might aim to **appeal** to audiences by writing things that they know they'll **agree** with — e.g. most people buy a particular newspaper because they know it will express **similar views** to theirs. Journalists for that paper know what views will appeal to the audience and make them want to keep reading.

3) Writers might know their readership and try to **influence** or **change** their views in some way, e.g. charity adverts.

4) The meaning of a text can be **ambiguous**. Often the meaning expressed on a **literal** or **explicit level** is different to the one on a **figurative** or **implicit level** (see p.18). Writers can challenge readers to provide their **own** meanings.

5) For example, writers are sometimes **ambiguous** on **purpose**. They leave things **open** for the audience to **interpret**, e.g. in the film *Lost in Translation* (2003), a character whispers something to another character at the end. The audience never find out what he says, and it's left up to them to come to their own conclusion.

Readers Interpret Texts in different ways

Readers **draw on** their own **values** and **experiences** when they **approach** texts.

1) Just like writers, readers bring their individual **backgrounds** and **biases** to texts — each reader's interpretation will be slightly different.

2) A reader's response to a text depends on the influences of social factors like **education**, **religion**, **family** and **the media**. These factors create the reader's **ideological position**.

3) Interpretations of texts are also a **product** of the readers' **historical context**, e.g.

- *Dr Jekyll and Mr Hyde* is a **Victorian** novel about a man who appears to have two sides to his personality.
- The way it was **interpreted** by Victorian readers is quite **different** to the meanings that it's given now.
- When readers at the time first saw the words *shame* and *sin* in the novel, some of them assumed that Mr Hyde was Dr Jekyll's **homosexual lover**.
- This is because **Victorian readers** would have **viewed** such a relationship as shameful and sinful.
- Other readers associated the character with **Jack the Ripper**, a **murderer** who was plaguing London **at the time**.
- Modern readers might see the novel as exploring issues related to the **self**, e.g. good and evil, and are less likely to think of the Victorian interpretations.

"No Hyde — I don't know what's wrong with her, but I don't think that's helping."

Practice Questions

Q1 Give two examples of how a writer might express their personal opinions in a text.

Q2 Explain the different effects created by using a first person narrative or a third person narrative.

Q3 What factors can influence a reader's interpretation of a text?

Essay Question

Q1 Outline the main factors that can influence a writer producing a text.

Apparently, 'Lost in Translation' was actually lost in translation...

I kid you not. When the title was translated into Hebrew, Chinese and Spanish (in South America), it turned up as Lost in Tokyo instead. So there you go... little bit of Hollywood trivia for you there. And you thought English Language was going to be all about spelling and grammar and endless transcripts. Well it's not. It's actually cool and ultra-glamorous.

Sources and Exam Questions

These pages show you what to expect from an exam question on analysing written language. It's important to apply the different parts of analysis that you've learnt in this section methodically in order to get the best marks.

> 1) Study the following texts A - E. The texts illustrate different varieties of language use.
>
> Analyse and compare the language in these texts and discuss the various ways in which these texts could be grouped, giving linguistic reasons for your choice.
>
> *[48 marks]*

Text A — An extract from the novel *The Way of All Flesh* (1903), by Samuel Butler

Old Mr. Pontifex had married in the year 1750, but for fifteen years his wife bore no children. At the end of that time, Mrs. Pontifex astonished the whole village by showing unmistakeable signs of a disposition to present her husband with an heir or heiress. Hers had long ago been considered a hopeless case, and when on consulting the doctor concerning the meaning of certain symptoms she was informed of their significance, she became very angry and abused the doctor roundly for talking nonsense. She refused to put so much as a piece of thread into a needle in anticipation of her confinement and would have been absolutely unprepared, if her neighbours had not been better judges of her condition than she was, and got things ready without telling her anything about it. Perhaps she feared Nemesis, though assuredly she knew not who or what Nemesis was; perhaps she feared the doctor had made a mistake and she should be laughed at; for whatever cause, however, her refusal to recognise the obvious arose, she certainly refused to recognise it, until one snowy night in January the doctor was sent for with all urgent speed across the rough country roads. When he arrived he found two patients, not one, in need of his assistance. For a boy had been born who was in due time christened George, in honour of his then reigning majesty.

To the best of my belief George Pontifex got the greater part of his nature from this obstinate old lady, his mother - a mother who though she loved no one else in the world except her husband (and him only after a fashion) was most tenderly attached to the unexpected child of her old age; nevertheless she showed it little.

Text B — A film review of the *Sex And The City* movie, By Celia Walden

"Everything that happens tonight must stay in this room," said Sarah Jessica Parker to the several hundred guests at last night's world premiere of Sex And The City the movie.

But with the girlish excitement filling the cinema it seemed unlikely anyone would heed her plea.

Just in case none of us remember, the producers of the much-awaited film version of the hit TV series remind fans with a quick recap at the start of the film where the four characters were at the point we left them when the series ended.

Three years on, the two Ls are still carrying the storyline along: labels and love. In the first half-hour we're bombarded by so much brand placement that one might as well be witnessing an extended Vogue photo shoot brought to life.

While love scenes between the happy characters brought not so much as a murmur from the audience, a Vivienne Westwood dress and a Louis Vuitton handbag provoked coos of heartfelt admiration.

The triumph of capitalism is as unabashed as it always was but given, if possible, a greater ironic twist.

In 20 years, Carrie Bradshaw, the lovelorn journalist, has come a long way: she is engaged to a billionaire, who can offer her a walk-in wardrobe and more Manolos than she can ever dream of - but the consumer Cinderella has a crash heading her way.

And as the film progresses, the seemingly adult and perfect lives of the four fortysomethings start to show cracks.

Miranda's husband Steve commits an act she may never be able to forgive him for while Samantha's ego threatens to derail her relationship with Smith Jerrod.

Just Charlotte seems to have escaped the New York clique's curse.

It is only in the last 10 minutes that we find out whether the fairytale has the happy ending the audience so desperately seemed to crave. But one thing's for sure: fans of the series will lap this film up.

It was coarse, sentimental, and outrageously materialistic - just as we hoped and expected it would be.

The Daily Telegraph, 2008

Sources and Exam Questions

Text C — A web page for an educational children's club

| Who are We? | Teaching | Case Studies | Contact Us |

Why fish?
Instructors
Lessons
Links
Gallery

Welcome to Carp-ey Diem

Carp-ey Diem helps children master the ancient art of carp fishing, whilst building strong learning skills, boosting their confidence, and teaching them respect for nature.

We give your child:

- an opportunity to learn at their own pace
- a positive attitude
- confidence to meet new challenges
- invaluable experience

Realise your child's potential — Join in Now

Carp-ey Diem - teaching kids to fish since 1947

Carp-ey Diem

Text D — A competition entry form

CAPTION COMPETITION ENTRY FORM

Name
Address Line 1
Address Line 2
Town
Postcode
D.O.B

Please note — this competition closes at midnight on 25/08/2008

Your Caption

I declare that this caption has not been published elsewhere and that I am the original author

You may use my caption in advertising should it be declared the winner of the caption competition

*Please inform me if my caption is **not** successful (see over for Terms and Conditions)*

Send your entries to:
Caption Competition,
P.O Box 4653,
Sheepy Parva,
Nuntonshire,
NU88 9UN

Signed:

Text E — A self-diagnosis booklet

Insomnia is best known as the inability to get to sleep, but sufferers are also affected by being unable to stay asleep, or by waking up too early. Experiencing these effects for an extended period of time is called chronic insomnia, whilst short-term sufferers experience what's called transient insomnia.

Chronic Insomnia

You can take some measures to try and alleviate chronic insomnia (see page 17). If these fail to have the desired effect then it may be best to seek medical advice to try and isolate the causes of the sleeping disruptions. On occasions, chronic insomnia is one of the symptoms of depression, but there are also many other potential causes.

Transient Insomnia

Short term insomnia often remedies itself in the space of a few days. Usually it is nothing to worry about but if you start to experience excessive worry about not being able to sleep, and if this in turn keeps you awake, then you might want to seek medical advice. Ultimately though, transient insomnia is fairly common and could be caused by bereavement or stress in your professional or personal life.

Do Well in the Exam

For your AS exam, you'll need to understand language frameworks and linguistic concepts, know how to analyse different types of discourse, organise your answers, and write clearly and precisely. If that's all Greek to you, panic ye not. For here is a helpful little section, with some exam and coursework tips neatly crowbarred into a nutshell.

Make sure you know How To Get Marks

You need to think about the **assessment objectives** for the questions — these are the **criteria** the examiners use to mark your answers:

AO1	You get **AO1** marks for using linguistic terminology correctly and writing accurately.
AO2	You get **AO2** marks for applying linguistic approaches to questions, and showing that you understand issues related to the construction and analysis of meaning in texts.
AO3	You get **AO3** marks for analysing and evaluating the influence of context on the language used.

Basically, the examiners want you to show that you understand the way purpose, audience and context affect the ways that language is produced and received.

Make sure you know your Language Frameworks

Language frameworks can be thought of as **headings** to help you to **structure** your **analysis**. You need to be able to **identify them** in different kinds of texts and explain how the features are used to help the text **achieve its purpose**:

> **Language Frameworks**
>
> - **Lexis** (vocabulary)
> - **Semantics** (meanings that words convey)
> - **Grammar** (word classes and syntax)
> - **Phonology** (sounds)
> - **Pragmatics** (social conventions surrounding language use)
> - **Graphology** (visual appearance and arrangement of the text)
> - **Discourse** (how segments of language are developed and structured)

1)   You need to refer to as many of these as possible, as long as they're **appropriate**.

2)   Don't focus on just **one framework** and **ignore** the rest. For example, if you write a lot on graphology (in written discourse) or non-fluency features (in spoken), and don't get chance to mention grammar, you won't **score highly** on the mark scheme.

3)   Don't just be descriptive. You have to relate the frameworks to **meaning** and **purpose**,
     e.g. *The adjective 'unique' is persuasive [**purpose**], suggesting that the product is special [**meaning**].*

Think about how you're going to Approach the Questions

When you're analysing **non-topic-based discourse** in the exam (section A asks you to group texts according to features you think they share), think about the points on this checklist:

1)   Read the texts **quickly**, just to get a feel for what they're generally about. Then read them again **more carefully**, noting down what the **subject matter** is.

2)   For **written** texts, identify genre, register, the likely audience and purpose.

3)   For **spoken** texts, identify context, the role of the participants, register, pragmatics and conversational theory.

4)   Find **examples** of the language frameworks — be selective and **link** linguistic features to purpose and meaning.

Topic-based questions still give you a **text** to **analyse**, but your analysis has to focus upon a certain aspect of the text.

1)   This sort of question requires you to have a good knowledge of **particular language topics** (like power or gender) as well as being able to apply the language frameworks to the text.

2)   Look for features that **specifically relate** to the topic (e.g. power, gender, occupation, technology, etc.).

3)   The best way to prepare is to **underline key features** in the texts you're given so you can refer back to them when you're writing your answer.

AQA B Exam — Section A

The AS AQA B exam is called **Categorising Texts**.

The exam has Two Sections

The **AQA B** paper lasts **two hours** and is split into **two sections** — section A is a question on **text varieties** and section B is a topic-specific question on **language in social contexts**.

Section A — Text Varieties

1) This section contains **one** compulsory question.

2) You'll get about six **written** and **spoken** texts to analyse.

3) You'll have to discuss the various ways in which these texts can be **grouped together**.

4) You'll need to write about things like: **purpose**, **genre**, level of **formality**, **mode** (spoken, written, multimodal), **representation** and linguistic features (**lexis**, **grammar**, **phonology** and so on).

5) There are **48 marks** available for this question.

Think about how to Organise Your Answers

1) It helps if you go into the exam with a **clear idea** about how you're going to organise your answers.

2) There are various approaches you can take, as long as you're **methodical** and **thorough**. Here are some things to think about when you're preparing to answer the questions.

Written Discourse	Spoken Discourse
The first things to identify are:	Make sure you're familiar with the following:
Genre, purpose, register, formality, likely audience.	Context, content, function, participants.
Then to compare texts, write in **more detail** about:	Then to compare texts, write in **more detail** about:
Graphology (layout, fonts, use of visual stimuli)	**Phonology** (pronunciation features)
Phonology (alliteration, assonance, repetition)	**Non-fluency features** (pauses, false starts, fillers)
Lexis (lexical fields, figurative language)	**Non-verbal** aspects of speech (stress)
Grammar (word classes, e.g. modals, types of adverb)	**Pragmatics** (conversational theory)
Discourse structure (beginning, how it's developed, end)	**Lexis**, **grammar** and **discourse structure**

3) The exam board might include texts like adverts, conversations, websites, feature articles, comics, instructions or lists, and speech or radio transcripts. Here are a few ways that you could group some of the common texts.

- Adverts, websites and comics use a lot of **bold graphological features** to stand out and attract casual viewers.

- Comics, conversations, speeches and radio extracts can be grouped according to their representation of **spoken language** — they could show different levels of **formality** in the language choices, or be grouped because they represent features of **dialects** or **accents** in some way.

- Feature articles and comics are usually meant to **entertain**, but this can also be true of websites, adverts and instructions, depending on their **tone**, **formality** and use of **figurative language** or **phonetic features**.

Keep your answers Simple and Concise

1) Write **clearly** and **concisely** — don't try to impress the examiner with big words for the sake of it.

2) Write in **paragraphs** and make sure that each paragraph has a **clear focus** (e.g. grouping texts by a certain feature like lexis).

3) When quoting, make sure that you use **inverted commas**. It doesn't matter if these are single or double as long as you are **consistent**. For example — *the modal auxiliary 'might' adds a degree of uncertainty to whether the athlete will achieve what he has set out to do.*

4) Avoid using **long quotations**. It's much better to work quotations **into your sentences** rather than present them as big separate chunks.

AQA B Exam — Section B

*The second section of the exam is **topic-specific**.*

You have a choice of **Three Questions**

Section B — Language and Social Contexts

1) In this section you have to choose **one** question out of three.
2) The three questions are on **language and gender**, **language and power**, and **language and technology**.
3) In each case, you'll get **one text** (written, spoken or multimodal) that you'll analyse as part of the question.
4) There are **48 marks** available for this question.

You'll need to make sure you're **comfortable** talking about the following things for this section of the exam.

Gender — How gender is **represented** in texts and how the **roles** of men and women are portrayed in everyday life. How gender roles function and are **conformed** to or **subverted** in mixed and same-sex conversations.

Power — The way power is **communicated** in discourses, e.g. official letters or documents, medical advice, etc. How individuals **exert power** in interactions like arguments, debates or speeches, etc.

Technology — How language has been **changed** by mobiles, the Internet, etc., and how this has affected **social practices**

Here's an **Example Question** and **Answer** to give you some tips:

4) Read Text 1. How has the language of the text been influenced by technology?

Straight to the point, focusing on the impact of technology.

These text messages show some of the distinctive qualities of text messaging language. The language used is influenced by the need for participants to respond quickly with a limited set of buttons to work with.

Good range of examples, supporting the idea of simplification.

For this reason, words are abbreviated, as in *sis*, and spelling is simplified, as in *nite*. Another form of simplification occurs with the omission of vowels (*wkd, Lndn*) and with the dropping of final consonants (the final *g* is dropped in *goin, doin*, and *hangin*). There is one example where a single consonant is used to replace a consonant cluster (*athletix* rather than *athletics*). Silent vowels at the end of words are also omitted (*els*). In addition to simplified spelling, there are also examples of phonological spelling: *bin, wiv, nuffin, strick*.

Text 1 — text messages from the mobile phones of a 17-year-old boy and his 14-year-old sister.

Simon:	*hi sis,ows it goin down in Lndn?*
Trish:	*its cool.bin on the EYE*
Simon:	*wow bet that was wkd. wot els?*
Trish:	*nuffin much.bin hangin round wiv billy*
Simon:	*BILLY? aw billy, hes well cool.*
Trish:	*yeh*
Simon:	*he still doin athletix?*
Trish:	*yeh,really into it.trains every nite almos*
Simon:	*hows auntie Bett? lol.*
Trish:	*lol shes really strick. we don't get away wiv nuffin not even Billy n hes nearly 16*

Colloquial expressions such as *ows it goin?, wkd* (wicked), *hangin round*, and *well cool* suggest an informal conversation between two people who are comfortable with each other. Grammatical structures are incomplete, especially with the omission of personal pronouns: *[I] bet that was wkd*, or subject-verb combinations: *[I've] bin on the EYE*.

Comments on lexical / grammatical frameworks with examples.

The text conversation mirrors some features found in actual spoken conversation. There is an opening sequence with Simon addressing his sister with *hi* and her responding. Brother and sister take turns with Simon driving the conversation forward by asking questions. However, there are also declaratives, particularly from Trish, who tells her brother about Billy's athletics training and the strictness of her aunt.

Comments on conversational features of text messaging.

This is quite a good answer. It **focuses** on the **question**, identifies a **range** of **features** and gives some **good examples**. It explores how text messaging has some of the same features as **spoken conversation** and shows that the student is aware of the **context**.

The student could **improve** the answer by writing about the **function** of the **interaction**, and how the exchanges might fit in with **conversational theory**. If it carried on like this, the essay would get at least **32 marks** out of **48**.

AQA B Coursework — Writing Texts

What the Exam Board Wants

For your AQA B coursework, you have to do **two** different pieces of **original writing**.
They have to be from different genres and written for a different purpose and audience.

The total length for the two pieces together is 1500 - 2500 words. You can pick a type of text from any of the following areas:	
A text to entertain	• an extract from an interview • part of a script from a TV show • a parody or piece of satirical writing
A text to inform	• news coverage of an important event • a piece of travel writing • a press release from a football club
A text to instruct	• a step-by-step fitness regime • a manual for a computer game • a novice's guide to email (or similar)
A text to persuade	• a film, music, car or restaurant review • a political speech • a piece of motivational speaking

Check the coursework tasks with your teacher — there's a chance they might change.

If you need some help, have a look at:

• Section 2 (terminology and useful language features, p.16-31).

• Section 4 (language in different contexts, e.g. the media and exerting power, p.46-57).

• Section 5 (e.g. if you're doing a script, refer to features of spoken language, p.60-65).

• Section 6 (written language, purpose, genre and representation, p.68-77).

You also have to submit **two commentaries** in total — one for **each** piece of writing (see p.84).
The **total** word count for the **two** commentaries together is **1000 words**.

Each type of text shares some Common Features

Here are some hints on the main features to include. For more on these features, see Section 6.

1) Entertainment Texts

You can write in several different styles if you pick an entertainment text, but they all share some features:
• **Structure** — Most entertainment texts have a **fairly complex** structure. For example, a novel usually has a **sophisticated plot line**, and plays need **stage directions** as well as lines for the characters.
• **Language** — a written entertainment text usually has quite complex language and lots of **figurative devices**. Spoken and written entertainment texts sometimes use **non-standard** language to **subvert convention**.

2) Informative Texts

Informative texts may be **factually based**. Make sure your **facts** are right and the language is **appropriate**.
• **Structure** — the bulk of the facts you want to get across should be in the **middle** of the **text**. Have a more general introduction and conclusion to **frame** what you're talking about.
• **Language** — it's important that your language **suits** your **target audience**. If you're writing to inform **children**, you'll have to use quite different language to what you'd use in a text written for your friends or parents.

3) Instructional texts

If you write a set of instructions, you need to guide a reader through the text, step by step.
• **Structure** — you'll probably need to use numbered or bullet-pointed **lists**. The reader can't go on to the next one until they've **completed** everything the former one tells them to do — they're very **linear**.
• **Language** — instructions are usually **imperative sentences** (see p.15). Sometimes the word choices are **specific** to the type of task or process that the reader is doing.

4) Persuasive texts

The best persuasive texts manage to get the reader to 'buy into' the idea they're promoting.
1) **Structure** — it's best to steadily **build** your **argument** as you go along and end with an **emphatic conclusion**.
2) **Language** — persuasive texts are meant to be **emotive**, so use lots of **direct address** and **inclusive pronouns**, as well as **emotive adjectives** to promote your subjective judgements.

AQA B Coursework — Writing Commentaries

*Commentaries are where you get the chance to **explain** the language choices you made in your **coursework**.*

Writing a **Commentary** shows your choices were **Intentional**

1) The commentary shows the examiner that you knew what you were doing in the **writing process**, and that you've thought about the effect that your **language choices** have had on the piece of writing you produced.

> **Your commentary is a review of what you've done and how you did it.**
> It will refer to all or some of the following frameworks, depending on the kind of text.
> **Lexis, semantics, grammar, phonology, pragmatics, graphology** and **discourse structure**.

2) You need to keep to the point and make sure you discuss all the features **equally**.

3) Your commentary should explain how your language choices in your coursework **match** the genre, mode, purpose, audience and subject matter of your text.

4) It should also discuss how planning and reworking has affected the final text, and how what you've written has been influenced by other texts.

5) Commentaries should be **400-500** words.

Your commentary should be **Concise and Well-Organised**

Start by stating what **kind of text** you've written, who it's **aimed at**, and what its **purpose** is. For example:

> I chose to write the kind of unsolicited letter that charitable organisations send out to the public. The purpose of this letter is to persuade adults to donate money to a good cause; in this case, a campaign to end forced child labour in developing countries.

Now describe some of the **specific language choices** you made, making sure that you always refer back to how they helped you **identify with** and get your **message across** to the audience. Here are a few examples of the kind of things you should be aiming to write about:

Mentioning narrative voice is a good way to describe how you're treating the reader.

> Throughout the letter I used the second person pronoun *you* to address the reader directly. By doing this, I aimed to involve the reader by making it seem I was talking to them personally...

Try to describe how you've attempted to manipulate the reader's response to the text.

> Another technique I used for involving the reader was incorporating a number of rhetorical questions, e.g. *Can we stand by and let this happen?*, and *Would you let this happen to your own child?*. My purpose here was to further personalise the issue and involve the reader by projecting the situation onto their lives...

Discuss the lexis you've used, and why you've chosen certain words (e.g. for their connotative meaning).

> To further the personal impact of the text, some of the lexis I used was deliberately emotive as I wanted the reader to be shocked by what they read. For this reason, I gave a short case study of a six-year-old boy called Arjit. I used adjectives such as *fatherless, unloved* and *malnourished* to give a sense of his vulnerability, loneliness and frailty. I also used the metaphor *dungeon* to describe the factory where Arjit works to emphasise that his workplace is a dark, harsh and restricted environment...

Grammar can be just as influential as lexis on the tone and style of a text, so make sure you discuss it. Also consider how the complexity of the sentences and words make your text accessible to your reader.

> I mainly used simple sentences because it gives the text a shorter, more dynamic tone, making it more assertive and therefore more persuasive. As this is a letter that someone might easily throw away without reading, it was important that the opening sentences in particular were short and to the point, e.g. the very first sentence, which simply states that *Two hundred children died last year.* This is a stark fact and grabs the reader's attention straight away...

Describe how you've organised your text.

> The letter has a clear structure. First I paint a picture of the situation focusing on Arjit, then broaden the text to show how forced labour is a worldwide issue which affects thousands of children. Finally, having hopefully influenced the reader, I have urged them to donate money, using modals and adverbs of time to give a sense of urgency: *You **must** do something **now**!*

You might want to talk about how the structure reflects or subverts the conventions of the genre you've chosen to write in.

> There are **two** important things to remember.
> 1) **Support** every point you make with **examples**.
> 2) For every linguistic choice you discuss, say how it **affects** the **audience** or contributes to the **effect** of the text.

Answers to Exam Questions

This answer section gives you some tips about what to include when you have a go at the sample exam questions at the end of sections three to seven. We haven't written entire essays (everyone writes essays differently), but these points are just suggestions for the kinds of things you should think about including in your answers.

Section Three — Varieties of English
Pages 42-45

The question asks you to discuss the sources in terms of the varieties of English used, and how they could be grouped. Here are some points you could make in your answer:

Dialect

- Text B contains dialect words like *nowt* and *mardy*, which suggest that the teenagers are speaking a regional dialect.

- It also contains non-standard grammar, which is a feature of regional dialects (*she didn't do nowt wrong*, *that don't even make sense*).

- The speakers in text B miss out the definite article *the* in constructions like *she was gonna meet him at pub*. This grammatical feature is mostly specific to the Yorkshire dialect, so this is probably where the speakers are from.

Sociolect

- In text B the speakers are a group of teenagers who are friends, so their sociolect is made up of informal, familiar language. This is shown by speaker A's use of the address term *mate*. Their language also includes a lot of slang words, like *minging*, *chucked* and *snogging*, and elision in words like *wanna* and *dunno*. Their language contains informal fillers typical in teenagers' language, e.g. *innit though right* and *like*.

Idiolect

- In text B, Speaker B's idiolect is evident in their use of *well* as an intensifier (*he's well fit, he can be well horrid*).

- In text A, Lord Augustus's idiolect in text A is evident in his use of ellipsis — he misses out the third person pronoun *she* in these clauses: *Knows perfectly well what a demmed fool I am — knows it as well as I do myself*.

Occupational Sociolect

- Text E is a cooperative interaction, with feedback features and turn-taking. However, there's an obvious hierarchy between the speakers, which is often evident in language of the workplace. Speaker A appears to be in authority over B — A addresses him with his first name a lot: *have a look at the v5 Greg*, also using an imperative in this example. A invites B to take control, but then speaks for him, which suggests that A is in charge.

- The lexical field contains references to cars and specific car parts (*two point five diesel, MAF, rev limiter*). Much of the lexis is context-specific jargon — it's referential and deictic (*that coupe*). This is a quick, efficient way for A and B to communicate.

- The problem with A and B's jargon is that the customer is left behind and hardly figures in the conversation, other than when invited to answer questions. It's clear from the customer's use of fillers, hedging and pauses that they don't really understand. Rather than explaining the jargon, A uses this to avoid having to answer the question of when the car will be finished, simply replying *a bit of Forté will do it*.

- Text C also contains occupational sociolect and jargon, e.g. *uPVC Georgian Hip, box gutter* and *fascia board*. The

employees use it to communicate quickly and concisely. Unlike the jargon in text E, this is appropriate to the situation because it doesn't exclude any non-specialists. The specialists need to use it for their specific needs.

- The sociolect in text C contains examples of general business language, e.g. *usual practice*. It also contains words that are specific to this occupational field, e.g *abutment*, and words that are specific to the particular company, e.g. *149 starting handbook*. This lexis is part of the employees' occupational sociolect — it's specific to the situation they are in.

- Text D also contains specific technical language, but it is for people who are part of the same interest group, rather than the same occupational group. This sociolect contains lexis from the semantic field of food, and there are lots of detailed descriptions of particular dishes: *ham hock and parsley terrine, lavender and Ossetra caviar*. The text assumes knowledge from the readers, so it doesn't explain technical terms like *palate* or *haute cuisine*.

- Text D contains features that are typical with language that describes food, e.g. French loan words such as *confit* and *sommelier*, and lots of premodifiers: *poached line-caught turbot*.

- The function of text C is to obtain and impart information, so it contains mostly declarative sentences, with one clear interrogative: *Just wondering if the guarantee covers this?* The ellipsis in this question is evidence of some of the features of spoken language in the text. Omitting *I was* also makes the question more concise and to-the-point, which fits with the purpose of the email. Because the text is purely functional, it contains short sentences and doesn't have a complex syntax. Graphologically the layout of the email means that the information is presented clearly — the previous email is there for reference, and information like the date and time is separate from the main text.

- In contrast, the function of text D is to entertain and persuade, as well as to inform. Because of this, it contains a more varied and colourful lexis: *globs, chilliness*, and lots of adjectives: *sharp and tangy*. The syntax is complex, with lots of subordinate clauses. It is designed to entertain and impress the readers.

Standard English

- Text A is an extract from a play script, so the language is more structured and contains fewer non-fluency features than the spontaneous speech in text B. In contrast to the speakers in text B, the characters in this extract use mostly Standard English, e.g. *It is an awfully dangerous thing*. The writer may have used this as a literary device to suggest that the characters are well-educated or upper-class. This is supported by the fact that one of the characters has a title — *Lord Augustus*.

Formality

- You can tell that Text A is an informal conversation between friends because of the use of informal address terms like *my dear boy* and affectionate nicknames like *Tuppy* and *Dumby*.

- In text A, words like *hallo*, and modifiers like *awfully* and *perfectly* would have been considered informal at the time the play was written, although they seem quite formal to readers today. The text also contains some non-standard slang words like *demmed* and *monstrous*.

- The lexis in text E is also informal and colloquial, as expected in spontaneous speech (*we've had a bit of a problem with it really*). Speakers A and B use more formal language with the customer than they do with each other, e.g. A uses a less direct request with the customer: *if you'd just like to come through*

Answers to Exam Questions

here, than is used with B: *do you want to take him through to have a look*.

- Emails are multimodal texts — they contain aspects of spoken and written language. This is evident in text C, which contains some informal language that you might expect in spoken interaction, e.g. *give me a shout*, and deictic expressions like *Hi*.

- Texts C and D are different to texts A and B because they have a very specific function, rather than just a social one, so the lexis is more technical. They are also different to text E because they are written texts. The language is mostly formal and Standard English is used. Unlike texts A, B and E, there aren't any slang or dialect features. Text D can be grouped with text A because they are both crafted to entertain an audience.

Section Four — Language in Social Contexts
Pages 58-59

1 **Conversation between a manager and two trainees**
The question asks you to analyse a spoken discourse between three people — a manager, a male trainee and a female trainee, in relation to the significance of gender in the interaction. Below are a list of language and gender issues that you should aim to cover in your answer:

- The function of the conversation is referential. The manager provides information and guidelines to the two trainees.

- The context is one where language reveals the power relations between the three speakers involved. The manager speaks the most, followed by the male trainee, then the female trainee. This shows that the manager is the dominant speaker in the conversation, and holds most of the power.

- The manager assumes control by virtue of their knowledge of how the shop operates and what is expected of the trainees. They use emphasis and repetition to reinforce this (*and I mean eight-thirty*). The manager also uses politeness strategies (*I'd like you to work*), in which the use of *I* personalises the manager's request, and probably makes it more likely to be respected by the trainees. The manager's speech also contains filled pauses like *erm* but this is more about creating time to think rather than being nervous.

- The male trainee is the more self-assured. He uses informal terms and slang (words like *cool*) and affirmatives like *sure* and *fine* to look for covert prestige. He asks questions and offers answers without being prompted. His informal language affects the amount of power the manager can assert.

- The male trainee also interrupts the manager at one point to talk about his work experience. This assumes control over the manager in the conversation, and suggests that he's a lot more confident than the female trainee. He offers the female trainee a lift to work, assuming a responsible / controlling role.

- In contrast, the female trainee is less self-assured. She hesitates and aims for overt prestige by using fillers like *yes* rather than *yeh*. Her filled pauses show that she is nervous. Her responses are more submissive, with back-channel noises like *mm*. When she attempts to explain her travel issues she is interrupted by the male trainee.

- Of the two trainees, the male is more dominant than the female. This seems to support Lakoff's deficit model.

- The role of the manager doesn't follow any traditional stereotypes, but their language use displays a lot of sexism, e.g. *growing lad like you, don't worry sweetheart*, and *little miss efficient*. This is patronising to the female trainee in particular.

- The lexical field relates to the service industry (*tills*) and working routines (*breaktimes, lunch time* and *eight-thirty*).

2 **Transcript of a Chemistry lesson**
This question asks you to look at power relationships. Here are some points you could include in your answer:

- The text takes place in a school classroom, so the environment is immediately more formal than that of a conversation between friends. The context means that there is an acknowledged leader of the interactions, the teacher, who you would expect to be the dominant speaker.

- The power relationships in this extract are most apparent in the address terms used by the speakers. The pupils address the teacher as *sir*, a sign of respect, while the teacher addresses them using their first names (*James, Tash*). This shows that is the authority figure.

- The teacher also shows his authority by using imperatives (*settle down, keep ties on*). As a politeness strategy, some orders are given as questions, but in the context of the school lesson the pupils understand that they're not supposed to respond and they don't have a choice, for example *can we to what we were doing last week*.

- The teacher uses direct questions (*what is it that happens to atoms*) to elicit a response from the pupils. He also uses the first person plural pronoun *we* to include them, and as an invitation that any of them can respond to his questions. This is common in educational sociolect. When no-one volunteers to answer, he directs questions at individuals to force them to respond (*what do they form (3.0) James*).

- In contrast the pupils use indirect questions to show respect (*sorry but erm (.) it's really hot in here sir (.) please may I*). This apologetic request to open the window involves lots of hedging, fillers, and false starts, which show that the pupil is uncomfortable about having to ask. The teacher's power is evident in his response — he uses the brief imperative *well open the window*.

- Power structures between the pupils are evident in their interaction. They try to act as a powerful group against the teacher — when one interrupts they all join in to disrupt the conversation as much as possible.

- However, it seems like pupil B is more disruptive than the other speakers, as he or she waits until someone else speaks before interrupting in to add an expression like *yeah*, or a non-standard phrase like *no one remembers nothing about this*.

- Pupils A and D seem more hesitant, although A is quite assertive at first when he or she interrupts the teacher to say *page ten*. However pupil A stumbles over language, e.g. *they don't (.) they don't* when put on the spot. Pupil D appears the least powerful, making a hesitant request to open the windows starting with an apology *sorry*.

- The teacher controls the discourse even though the pupils try to assert power by interrupting him and shifting the focus of the conversation. He uses repetition to bring it back to the subject he wants to discuss, e.g. by repeating *what happens to atoms*. Both pupil B and the teacher use tag questions to encourage the other to agree, (*didn't we, does it now*). These are used rhetorically to support their argument and force the other to agree.

3 **Chatroom conversation between two friends**
This question asks you to think about the impact of technology on the language used by two friends in a chatroom. Here are some points you could include in your answer:

Answers to Exam Questions

- The function of the chatroom conversation is mostly interactional, but it also has referential elements in which the speakers exchange information.

- As they're friends, and because they're talking in a chatroom, the speakers communicate very informally, using slang like *cool* and *dosh*.

- Technology has had a big impact on the language they use, stemming from a need to communicate quickly e.g. dropping vowels from words like *hw* (how), *havnt*, or *yr* (year) and having relatively limited options on a keyboard compared to spoken language). They use different typefaces from each other so that it will be easier to distinguish one participant in the conversation from the other.

- They use a range of linguistic features: phonetic spelling (*newayz*), non-standard use of punctuation marks, numbers for sounds (*l8tr*), numbers for words (*love 2*), phonetic spelling (*Cud do. Wat time*), emoticons (:'-(), symbols (*be ther @ 8*), upper case (*BRILL*).

- Sentences are often shortened and function words omitted (*hey rosie hw u doin?*).

- The conversation contains many of the features found in spoken interaction: an opening and closing sequence, adjacency pairs, turn-taking, question and answer and topic shifts, boyfriends, college, plans for the evening).

- Chatroom interaction is less spontaneous than regular conversation, e.g. one participant has plenty of time to decide if she wants to accept the other's invitation before replying.

Section Five — Analysing Spoken Language
Pages 66-67

1   The question asks you to analyse and compare the three source texts. Here are some features of each text that you might want to consider and use to contrast the texts in your essay:

Text A — conversation between a customer and newsagent

- The conversation has a transactional function — one speaker wants to buy a paper and find some odd jobs for his grandson. This can be seen from the fact that most utterances are either suggestions, questions or responses.

- The conversation contains features of informal, spontaneous speech, including dialect expressions (*now then*), slang (*cheers, mate*), ellipsis (*bit late delivering*), elision (*gonna*) and non-fluency features (*he's gonna need some er some work you see (.) while he's (.) but he doesn't drive*).

- It also contains deictic expressions that could only be understood in the specific context of the conversation (*I can put it up there with the others on the board over there*).

- The speakers use adjacency pairs and turn-taking rules, but there are also non-fluency features like self-corrections, false starts and hedging, which are common in spontaneous speech, e.g. *anyone in the village who might need (.) need a bit of work done*. They repeat each other a lot, which suggests they are in agreement.

- The speakers are on first name terms and use phatic conversation (*now then, comes round quick*) before B changes the subject. The control of the conversation mostly lies with A, as B is asking for information. B's speech contains pauses, fillers and hedging, as if he feels uncomfortable about asking for help, and so it might be a politeness strategy.

- In contrast, speaker A appears more confident, e.g. using the imperatives *write his name* and the phrase *tell you what*.

Text B — extract from a job interview

- The interviewer is overtly in charge straight away, opening the conversation with a rhetorical question and then an imperative (*come in, have a seat*). Taking control immediately sets the interviewer apart from the candidate who false starts straight away (*that's ri- (2.0) oh right*). This unequal power relationship continues throughout the interview as the interviewer regularly interrupts the candidate.

- An interview situation is always very formal despite being spontaneous speech — there aren't many contractions and there aren't any colloquialisms or non-standard grammatical features.

- The interviewer does give the candidate feedback and some back-channelling (*mmm-hmm*) to try and put them more at ease. They also let the candidate know when to speak by asking tag questions at the end of their utterances (*did you?*).

- There isn't much informal language in this extract. The language is standard English. There are some non-fluency features on the part of the candidate as they try to process the question and then answer it after being 'put on the spot' by the interviewer.

Text C — speech by a company director to company employees

- This is an official prepared speech, so it uses standard language and grammar throughout and is mostly very formal. The speaker has immediate prestige.

- The main content of the speech — the redundancy payments — is framed between two emotive apologies. This discourse structure shows that the speaker is delivering news that will directly affect the audience and has obviously been pre-planned with the delivery worked out in advance.

- Despite this, there is the occasional non-fluency feature and repetition of *I* and *can*. Most likely this is due to the awkward content of the speech, rather than any informality on the speaker's behalf.

- The speaker tries to appear as personable as possible by using collective addresses such as *you* and *hold our place*. This is also evident in the emotive language, such as *hurts* and *valued*, and the apologies that are repeated.

- The content is also emphasised by prosodic features as the underlined words like *no way* and *can't avoid* would be stressed in the actual delivery of the speech.

Section Six — Analysing Written Language
Pages 78-79

1   The question asks you to give various ways that texts A to E can be grouped. The texts are listed below with some of the linguistic features that you should try and focus on when comparing the texts and grouping them together.

Text A — Novel Extract — *The Way of All Flesh*

- **Purpose** — to entertain.
- **Audience** — readers of 19th century literature, and later students of English literature.
- **Genre** — literature, novel.
- **Register** — formal.
- **Lexis** — example of 19th century vocabulary, e.g. *disposition, confinement, Nemesis*.
- **Lexis** — references to context by use of *1750, George... reigning majesty*.

Answers to Exam Questions

- **Grammar** — complex sentences throughout.
- **Grammar** — use of parentheses and semicolons (also complex).
- **Tone** — serious yet with humorous undertones e.g. *who though she loved no one else in the world except her husband (and him only after a fashion).*
- **Narrator** — third person who interjects own personal views, e.g. *to the best of my belief* into narrative.
- **Representation** — depicts a strong woman (abusing the doctor and ignoring advice), though this also makes her seem ignorant when she is in fact pregnant.
- **Representation** — Her apparent inability to have children was considered a *hopeless case,* which reflects the domestic roles of women (i.e. producing children) at the time Butler was writing.

Text B — Film Review — *Sex and the City*

- **Purpose** — to inform / entertain
- **Audience** — predominately female (*girlish excitement*), those familiar with the TV series as the characters are mentioned by their first names.
- **Genre** — journalism, newspaper, review / critique
- **Register** —mostly standard English but the inclusive first person plural pronoun *we* adds to the chattiness / informality.
- **Lexis** — plenty of figurative language and lots of alliteration, e.g. *clique's curse, walk-in wardrobe, labels and love.*
- **Lexis** — field specific to the fashion industry, e.g. *Vogue, Louis Vuitton, Vivienne Westwood.*
- **Grammar** — mainly compound sentences, lots of punctuation to break up statements and make text less complex. Short paragraphs spread the content out over the page.
- **Narrator** — very subjective, giving opinions and displaying attitudes that the reader is expected to share, e.g. *just as we hoped.*
- **Representation** — represents film audience as females who might be attracted by the fashion labels mentioned (e.g. *coos of admiration*). Females in general are the focus of the review. This gives a certain representation of men as outside the text, and male characters in the film are only mentioned as props to the central characters' relationships.
- The cultural context is also represented by the author making the point that despite capitalism being very prevalent in the film it doesn't necessarily make the characters' lives better when they get what they want materially.

Text C — A web page for an educational children's club

- **Purpose** — to persuade.
- **Audience** — parents of young children.
- **Genre** — advertising.
- **Register** — formal.
- **Graphology** — lots of information in a small space, links to different parts of the website in frame and borders, separated by headings and bullet points. Stand-out link to *Join now.*
- **Graphology** — pictures to support information and act as persuasive images for parents / potential customers.
- **Graphology** — Logo for name of company indicates professionalism.
- **Lexis** — emphasises achievement and success, e.g. *learning skills, confidence, respect, invaluable experience.*
- **Grammar** — imperatives: *Realise your child's potential — Join in now.*

Source D — Entry form for a caption competition

- **Purpose** — to instruct.
- **Audience** — prospective competition entrants.
- **Genre** — entry form.
- **Graphology** — businesslike, with brief, essential text. Bold headings for sections that need to be filled in.
- **Grammar** — imperative sentences, e.g. *See over for Terms and Conditions, Send your entries to.*
- **Lexis** — no figurative or rhetorical language, only standard vocabulary and grammar.

Text E — Self-diagnosis booklet

- **Purpose** — to inform and instruct.
- **Audience** — adults concerned about health, specifically insomnia sufferers.
- **Genre** — medical, self-help.
- **Register** — formal.
- **Graphology** — headings to highlight subjects being discus e.g. *Transient Insomnia.*
- **Graphology** — short sentences and short paragraphs, so as to overload the audience with information.
- **Lexis** — specialist medical terminology e.g. *chronic, sympto depression.*
- **Tone** — reassuring, explains symptoms and treatment so the reader feels they have nothing to worry about.
- **Grammar** — use of second person *you* e.g. *you can take some measures,* to include the reader.

Glossary

abstract noun A **noun** that refers to a concept, state, quality or emotion.

accent The distinctive way an English speaker from a particular region pronounces words.

acronym A new word made from the initial letters of all the words in a name or **phrase**.

active voice When the **subject** of the sentence is directly performing the **verb**, e.g. *Steve burst the bubble.*

adjective A class of words that can appear before (attributive) or after (predicative) a **noun** or noun phrase to describe it.

adverb A class of words that modify **verbs** according to time, place, manner, frequency, duration or degree.

affixation The process of adding an affix before (**prefix**) or after (**suffix**) an existing word to change either its meaning or grammatical function.

alliteration When two or more words close to each other in a **phrase** begin with the same consonant sound.

anaphora When a word, usually a pronoun, refers back to something or someone that has already been mentioned, e.g. *Barrie can't come because he's ill.*

antithesis Type of **rhetorical language** where contrasting ideas or words are balanced against each other, e.g. *it's just too good from Green, and just too bad for the goalkeeper.*

antonyms Words with opposite meanings.

article A kind of **determiner** that shows if the reference to a **noun** is general (*a / an*) or specific (*the*).

aspect A **verb's** aspect shows whether the action it refers to is already completed, or if it is still taking place.

assimilation When sounds next to each other in a spoken word or **sentence** are pronounced in a similar way to make them easier to say.

assonance When the main vowel sounds of two or more words that are close together in a text are similar or the same.

audience A person or group of people that read, view or listen to a text. A writer or speaker can aim to reach a certain type of audience by using specific literary techniques and language choices.

auxiliary verbs Verbs used before the **main verb** in a sentence to give extra information about it, e.g. *I have seen him.*

back-channelling A kind of **feedback** in spoken language that supports the person speaking and shows that what is being said is understood.

blending When parts of two words are combined to make a new one, e.g. *netizen.*

buzz words Words that are fashionable in a particular occupational group.

cataphora A reference in a text to something in the future, that follows in later **phrases** or **sentences**, e.g. *These are the directions...*

characterisation The way that a writer conveys information about a character relating to their appearance, speech, etc.

clause The simplest meaningful unit of a **sentence**.

cliché A **figurative** expression that has lost its novelty value due to being overused.

clipping When a shortened version of a word becomes a word in its own right.

cohesion The linking of ideas in texts to ensure the text makes sense.

coining The general term for creating new words.

collective noun A **noun** that refers to groups of people, animals or things, e.g. *team.*

collocation Words that commonly appear together in order, in specific lexical units, e.g. *done and dusted.*

common noun A **noun** that refers to a class of things or a concept. Every noun is a common noun except those that refer to unique things, e.g. the names of particular people or places.

comparative An **adjective** that makes a degree of comparison, normally by adding an *-er* **suffix**, e.g. *faster.*

complement A word or **phrase** that gives more information about the **subject** or **object** in a sentence, e.g. *the boy is [actually a cow].*

compound A new word created by combining two or more existing words or **morphemes**.

concrete noun A **noun** that refers to things you can physically touch or see, e.g. *chair.*

conjunction A linking word that connects **phrases** and **clauses** to each other to form **sentences**.

connotation The associations that are made with a particular word.

context The circumstances that surround a word, **phrase** or text.

conversion When a word becomes part of a different **word class** in addition to its original sense (e.g. *message* is now both a **noun** and a **verb**).

coordinate clause An independent **clause** that's linked to another independent **clause** in the same **sentence**.

Glossary

count noun **Nouns** that can be preceded by a number and counted as plurals, e.g. *one book*, *two books* etc.

declarative A **sentence** that makes statements.

deixis A reference to something outside of the text or conversation that can't be understood unless you know the **context**.

demonstratives Words that refer to specific objects that only those involved in the discourse can see. They can be **pronouns**, e.g. *I like this*, or **adjectives**, e.g. *I like this bike*.

denotation The literal meaning of a word.

determiners Words that go before a **noun** to give information about what it's referring to, e.g. general or specific, how many there are, or to show possession.

dialect The distinctive **lexis** and **grammar** of a person's spoken English.

dialogue Any exchange between two or more characters or speakers.

difference model Tannen's (1990) theory about gender and conversation which states that men and women have different objectives when they interact.

discourse An extended piece of written or spoken language.

dominance model Zimmerman and West's (1975) theory that gender differences in conversations are due to male dominance in society.

double negative When negatives are used twice in a phrase, e.g. *I didn't do nothing*.

elision When sounds or **syllables** are slurred together in speech to make pronunciation easier and quicker.

ellipsis When part of a grammatical structure is left out of the **sentence** without affecting the meaning.

Estuary English An **accent** that was originally from the Thames Estuary area in London but is now heard outside the area and may be replacing RP as the country's most widespread form.

euphemism A word that is used as a substitute for harsher or more unpleasant sounding words or concepts.

exclamative A **sentence** that has an expressive function and ends with an exclamation mark.

exophoric reference Referring to something outside a text, e.g. *that* tree over *there*.

feedback Verbal and **non-verbal** signs that a person is listening to a speaker.

field The subject of a conversation. Contains specific **lexis** relating to that topic.

figurative language Language that is used to create images and emotions in a text.

filler A sound produced by speakers to keep a conversation going and avoid silence.

genre A group of texts with a particular form or purpose.

grammar The system of rules that govern how **phrases**, **clauses** and **sentences** are put together.

grapheme The smallest unit of writing that can create contrasts in meaning, e.g. individual letters or symbols.

graphology The study of the appearance of a text, how it looks on the page and how the layout helps get the meaning across.

head word A word that has the same grammatical function as the **phrase** that has been built around it, e.g. in a noun phrase, the head word is a **noun**.

hedging Word choices that show uncertainty in conversations, e.g. *probably*, *maybe*.

hyperbole When exaggeration is used for effect.

hypernym A general word that is a term for many **hyponyms**, e.g. *vehicle* is a hypernym of *car*, *bus*, *lorry*, etc.

hyponym A word that refers to a specific type of a **hypernym**, e.g. *car*, *bus*, *lorry* are hyponyms of *vehicle*.

ideology A set of ideas and beliefs.

idiolect An individual's **accent** and **dialect** features, as a result of their personal upbringing and experiences.

imagery Describing aspects of a scene to create a picture of it in the mind of an audience.

imperative A **sentence** that gives orders, advice or directions. It starts with a **main verb** and doesn't have a **subject**.

implication When a meaning is suggested, rather than explicitly described.

infinitive The base form of a **verb**, preceded by *to*.

inflection An **affix** that is attached to words to change the **grammar** of a sentence.

interrogative A sentence or utterance that asks a question.

intertextuality When a text makes reference to another existing text for effect.

intonation The pitch and tone of a speaker's voice, e.g. rising intonation shows it's a question.

Glossary

jargon Specialist words that are used by a particular social or occupational group that may not be understood by a non-member.

juxtaposition The way that parts of a text are arranged next to each other (e.g. text and image) to create certain effects.

lexis A general term for the words of a language.

liaison When a normally silent final consonant is pronounced between words or **syllables** to make them run together.

loan words Words that are taken from other languages.

main verbs Words that identify the action of a **sentence**.

management speak A way of communicating in the workplace designed to sound up-to-date and formal, but usually overly complex.

manner The level of formality in the relationship between two speakers and its effect on their social behaviour.

mass noun **Nouns** that can't be counted and don't have a plural (e.g. *information*).

metaphor Words or phrases that describe something as if it actually was something else, e.g. the *heart* of the matter.

metonymy Using a part of something, or one of its attributes, to describe the whole thing, e.g. *the press* to refer to journalists and the news industry.

modal auxiliary verbs Verbs that give more information about the **main verb**, but can't occur as main verbs themselves, e.g. *can*, *will*.

mode A way of classifying texts (e.g. written or spoken or a combination of different media).

monologue The utterances of one speaker or performer to an audience.

monosyllabic Words with only one **syllable**.

multimodal A text that involves elements of different **modes**, e.g. written, spoken, multimedia etc.

narrative voice The point of view from which written texts are described. Narrators can be first person, telling the reader directly about their experiences, or third person omniscient, describing the thoughts and feelings of all the characters.

neologisms New words, often created by advances in things like technology and science.

noun A word used as the name of a person, place, thing or concept.

object The part of the **sentence** that the **verb** acts upon, e.g. in *I broke a plate*, the plate is the object and ends up *broken*.

onomatopoeia A word that sounds like the noise it's describing.

oxymoron A phrase that brings two conflicting ideas together, e.g. *bittersweet*.

paralinguistic features Gestures or facial expressions that emphasise words or phrases in spoken communication.

parallelism The repetition of bigger structural features like a verse or image through a text.

parody Subverting traditional expectations of a text's features to produce humour or satire.

passive voice When the state of the **object** is described first, rather than the action of the **subject** (e.g. *the bubble was burst by Steve*).

personification When an object or situation is given human qualities.

phatic language Expressions that have a sociable function rather than a literal meaning.

phoneme The smallest unit of sound that can create a contrast in meaning.

phonology The study of the sound systems of languages, in particular the patterns of sounds.

phrase A meaningful unit of language built around a **head word**.

polysyllabic Words with more than one **syllable**.

post-modifier Words that come after the **head word** in a **phrase**, that tell you something about it.

pragmatics The study of how language functions in social situations.

pre-modifier Words used before the head word of a **phrase** (often **determiner** + **adjective**) that tell you something about it.

prefix An **affix** that comes before the base form.

preposition A word that defines the relationship between words in terms of time, space or direction, e.g. *the toy was in the box*, *he's behind you*.

primary auxiliary verbs **Auxiliary verbs** that can also occur as **main verbs** (*do*, *be* and *have*).

pronoun A word that can take the place of a **noun**.

proper noun A **noun** that is the name of a specific person, place or brand.

prosody **Non-verbal** aspects of speech like pace, stress, pitch, intonation, volume and pauses.

pun Replacing a word or phrase with one that sounds the same or similar for creative or humorous effect.

Glossary

Received Pronunciation An **accent** traditionally associated with educated people and the upper class. It's characterised by lots of long vowels and the pronunciation of /h/ and /t/ in words where most people with regional accents would not pronounce them.

referential language Spoken language that refers to objects around the speakers.

register Any of the different varieties of language used in different situations.

representation How the characters, narrator and writer are portrayed to an **audience**, in terms of how they behave and what they believe in.

rhetorical language Language with phonological or structural features used to provide extra effects or meanings.

semantics The study of how the meanings of words are structured and interpreted.

sentence An independent grammatical unit made up of one or more **clauses**.

similes Comparisons that use the words *like* or *as*.

slang Informal, non-standard vocabulary and casual speech.

sociolect A variety of language used by a particular social group.

Standard English A **dialect** of English considered 'correct' and 'normal', because it has distinctive and standardised features of spelling, vocabulary and **syntax**. It's the form of English usually used in writing.

sub-genre A group of similar texts that combine with others to create a complete **genre**.

subject The focus of a **sentence** — the person or thing that performs the action described by the **verb**.

subordinate clause A **clause** that gives extra information about the main clause, but can't stand alone and still make sense.

subtext The meaning behind what's actually being said or described.

suffix An **affix** that comes after the base form.

superlative An **adjective** that states the **noun** it's describing is beyond comparison, usually by adding -*est*, e.g. *fastest*.

syllables A word's individual units of pronunciation.

symbolism When a word or phrase represents something other than its literal meaning.

synonyms Words that have similar meanings.

syntax The grammatical rules about how words can be combined and work around each other in **sentences**.

tag question A question added to the end of a statement to encourage a response, e.g. *don't you think so?*

tense Grammatical **inflections** that show the time of the action, e.g. in the past or present, that the **verb** in a **sentence** took place.

transactional language Spoken exchanges aimed at making some sort of deal.

turn-taking A feature of orderly conversations when the chance to speak switches back and forward between the participants.

unresponsiveness A negative way of asserting control in conversations, either by withholding feedback or ignoring the other speaker entirely.

verb A class of words that describe the action or state that a **sentence** refers to.

word classes How words are categorised according to the function they can perform in a **sentence**.

Index

Index